THE NEW CITY HOME

THE NEW CITY HOME

SMART DESIGN FOR METRO LIVING

LESLIE PLUMMER CLAGETT

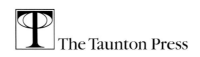

The Taunton Press

The Taunton Press
Inspiration for hands-on living™

Text © 2002 by Leslie Plummer Clagett
Photographs © 2002 by davidduncanlivingston.com (except where noted below)
Illustrations © 2002 by The Taunton Press, Inc.

Printed in Singapore
10 9 8 7 6 5 4 3 2 1

The Taunton Press, Inc., 63 South Main Street, PO Box 5506,
Newtown, CT 06470-5506
e-mail: tp@taunton.com

Distributed by Publishers Group West

Jacket design: Chen Design Associates
Interior design: Chen Design Associates
Layout: Susan Fazekas
Illustrator: Martha Garstang Hill
Photographer: davidduncanlivingston.com (except p. 178 bottom,
courtesy Morgante-Wilson Architects)

Library of Congress Cataloging-in-Publication Data
Clagett, Leslie.
   The new city home : smart design for metro living / Leslie Plummer Clagett.
     p. cm.
   ISBN 1-56158-461-4
   1. Architecture, Domestic--United States. 2. Architecture, Domestic--United States--
20th century. 3. Interior architecture--United States. 4. Apartment houses--Remodeling--
United States. 5. City and town life--United States. I. Title.
NA7208 .C58 2002
728'.31'0973091732--dc21
                                                        2001054186

The following manufacturers/names appearing in *The New City Home* are
registered trademarks or servicemarks: AstroTurf, DishDrawer, Dramamine,
Energy Star, Equator, Fisher & Paykel, General Electric, Homasote, Lincoln
Logs, Miele, Plycem, Spacemaker, Spray 'n Wash, and Sub-Zero.

To my family

ACKNOWLEDGMENTS

While it's a traditional term in making books, "acknowledgments" falls perfunctorily short of describing the debts owed to the many people involved in creating a project of this scope. My sincere thanks to all those who contributed to *The New City Home:*

- The homeowners who graciously opened their doors to us;

- The architects who provided both artistic vision and insight;

- The team at The Taunton Press, who with care and skill gave shape to the words and images on these pages: editors Peter Chapman, Carol Kasper, and Suzanne Noel; art director Paula Schlosser; publicity manager Ellen Williams; marketing manager Allison Hollett; and publisher Jim Childs;

- Photographer David Duncan Livingston, a very good friend with a very good eye;

- And John Clagett, who kept the light shining while stepping selflessly into the breach.

This book went to press in the aftermath of the 11 September 2001 attack on the World Trade Center. To many people, the twin towers symbolized the resourcefulness and perseverance of the city and its citizens. As a New Yorker, I pay tribute to their spirit.

CONTENTS

INTRODUCTION

The metropolis is heady with architectural contrasts: the collisions between big and not-so-big structures, edifices new and old, ornate and ordinary designs, glass and masonry and steel, good buildings and bad. The large-scale cacophony that's so stimulating on a sensory level can prove to be destabilizing when it comes to making a home in the city. Toward the goal of making this book informative as well as inspiring, I've worked to make it a realistic road map to design dilemmas while mirroring the diversity that's typical of urban areas.

For a start, there's a geographic balance to the content. While the traditional big-city bases— Boston, Philadelphia, and of course New York, Chicago, and Los Angeles—are covered, the book also features an itinerary of other locations. New Orleans, Toronto, Baltimore, Richmond, Portland, Montreal, and Minneapolis are just some of the cities included that confirm that the boom in downtown living isn't restricted to multimillion population centers.

Rather than focusing on a single housing type, a full menu of homes is represented. In addition to an assortment of high-rise apartments, town houses, and lofts, I also look at some more offbeat abodes, such as a converted auto shop and a former stable.

While the artistic appeal of the homes is of a constant caliber, this book provides a broader and deeper picture than is typically found. Instead of adopting a "fait accompli" point of view, I go behind the scenes to identify the impetus behind each project, examining how the design was developed. Responding to the needs of growing families and empty nesters, of wheelchair users and

full-time home workers, these residences display a high standard of both aesthetics and ingenuity.

Living in such a compressed context engenders its own set of day-to-day difficulties, and this book supplies a battery of city-tested solutions. From tips on the fine art of maximizing storage space to dealing with the ever-present noise, each chapter has a special section that focuses on a specific issue of urban living.

Whether you're already at home in the metropolis or contemplating a move there, *The New City Home* can help you create your personal space in an impersonal place.

 *part 1*

back to the city

From the Iron Age to the age of the Internet, the city has always both absorbed and promoted change. It thrives on reinvention. Today, the North American city is enjoying an upswing in popularity. With crime rates plummeting and budget surpluses being poured into community assets, cities are again meccas for culture and business—and residential use. No longer are downtowns deserted at the end of a workday or on weekends, partly because fewer people are commuting out to the suburbs.

Take a look at the numbers. (They'll give you a clue as to why you can never get a seat on the bus.) In the last decade of the 20th century, 75 percent of what the U.S. census defines as major metropolitan areas—the 218 locales with at least 100,000 residents—have increased their citizenry substantially, some as much as 135 percent. Across Canada and the United States, 35 cities now have populations of a half-million or more, with another 13 on the threshold. Who makes up this boon and what's at the root of the attraction?

THE URBAN RENAISSANCE

For a long time, the scenario went something like this: Young singles find a job in the big city, work there a while, get married, and in short order head out to the 'burbs to rear their kids. In recent years, though, people have bucked the small-town pattern set by their parents and have stayed put, moving upward in the urban housing market as their needs shift from renting a studio to owning family-size quarters. Enticed by extensive cultural resources, expanded career opportunities, an exciting change of pace, substantial financial rewards, and the vitality engendered by a richly diverse community,

ABOVE Seen at street level as well as along the skyline, layers of architectural history give every city its distinctive character. From left: Chicago, New York, Baltimore, and Boston.

In recent years, people have bucked the small-town pattern set by their parents and have stayed put, moving upward in the urban housing market as their needs shift from renting a studio to owning family-size quarters.

they're putting down roots in the city. The continuing prosperity has also attracted a new group to the metropolis: affluent empty nesters who are inspired to shed the suburban life and its trappings for the creative ferment of the urban scene.

For their part, city planners and administrators have worked hard to make their home turf all the more enticing to prospective property owners. Enlightened urban-design strategies have made the most of natural assets; witness the successful waterfront/parkland developments in Minneapolis, Providence, and Portland, Oregon. Another tactic centers on rehabbing historic districts and buildings, the deals typically sweetened with tax credits and low-interest construction loans. Much of Charleston, South Carolina, and the splendid Art Deco structures of Miami were saved in this fashion; their commercial success has more than repaid the investments of city leaders.

Carefully managed business ventures can act as catalysts for emerging neighborhoods. Pike Place Market in Seattle gradually grew from being a strictly wholesale center for fish and produce into a lively blend of restaurants, shops, clubs, and residences. Polishing and pumping up arts facilities is a certain way to lure folks downtown. Pittsburgh's theater row is undergoing a revitalization; it now sports a playhouse designed by Michael Graves. In New Jersey, the new state center for the performing arts is at the heart of a resurgent Newark.

Paralleling these urban improvements, some of the "advantages" of the suburbs have come up short of their original promise. Ennui is rampant, architectural and otherwise. A numbing sameness typifies the housing stock. A similar boredom has beset the commercial sector, with malls and chain stores having supplanted Main

Street years ago. Unless a day of carpooling satisfies one's wanderlust and an evening at the local multiplex suffices for a night of culture, it can be a pretty dull experience. Perhaps the most ironic failure is sprawl, which condemns commuters to spend more time stuck in traffic and less time at home—a home that for many has become an economic millstone. When contrasted with the conveniences and excitement offered by the city, suburbia looks—to many people— more like Siberia.

THE CHALLENGE OF CITY LIVING

In spite of the attraction of city living, taking up residence in the city involves a series of sacrifices that, when experienced collectively, threaten to throw life off-kilter. The first things surrendered are space and privacy. Neighbors are just a few feet and floors apart, rather than buffered by well-groomed yards. The proximity of your bedroom window and the building next door can be eye-opening, to say the least. Under the scrutiny of doormen, delivery guys, casual acquaintances, and total strangers, privacy becomes fleeting.

Next to succumb is peace and quiet. It's jettisoned by the clangorous realities of round-the-clock living. Street cleaners and sanitation workers toil in a raucous, predawn collusion of crashing trash cans and grinding gears. The normal background din of traffic also regularly rises to the forefront.

Last to go is a leisurely pace. "You snooze, you lose" isn't just a cute couplet: Coveted sports tickets are scalped out from under you, a moment's hesitation can cost you the last parking spot on the block, and just-vacated apartments are snapped up before the ink in the real-estate section is dry. Time here isn't ticked off in conven-

CITIES ON THE RISE

Metro Area	Population (2000)	% Increase (since 1990)
New York	21,199,865	8.4
Los Angeles	16,373,645	12.7
Chicago	9,157,540	11.1
Washington, D.C. area	7,608,070	13.1
San Francisco Bay Area	7,039,362	12.6
Philadelphia	6,188,463	5.0
Boston	5,819,100	6.7
Detroit	5,456,428	5.2
Dallas/Fort Worth	5,221,801	29.3
Houston	4,669,571	25.2

Numbers are based on 2000 U.S. Census statistics for metropolitan area populations. Changes are measured from the 1990 Census.

ABOVE AND BELOW In urban centers, the concept of a front yard is uniquely transformed. From an upper-floor vantage (below), it's restricted to the view out the window. Going down to the busy sidewalk (above), connections are instantly broadened and immediate.

tional hours and afternoons; the metropolitan clock is ringed with an unforgiving series of New York minutes.

HALLMARKS OF THE NEW CITY HOME

Why on earth would you subject yourself to such daily stress? More to the point, where can an urban dweller reclaim the above-mentioned civilities? One word: home. It becomes a locus for regrouping, a place for self-expression as well as self-preservation. It's where you can screen out prying eyes but still enjoy the sun by drawing the translucent shades. Double-glazed windows allow you to shut out sonic intrusions and enjoy some music—or even blessed silence. Where it's possible to control personal space, a saner pace prevails. Residential design for city dwellers serves two purposes: Beyond basic shelter, it's an environmental statement of self.

The qualities important to the city home aren't all that different in kind from those found *ex urbis*. The need for them, though, differs in degree, owing to the compressed context of the metropolis. As personal space in an impersonal place, the home assumes heightened importance. Among the aesthetic ingredients needed to balance the equation are character, craftsmanship, nature, and efficiency.

Residential design for city dwellers serves two purposes: Beyond basic shelter, it's an environmental statement of self.

Character

If home in the city is equal parts refuge and release, its design must satisfy both soul and psyche while simultaneously affirming the owner's individuality. Because the emphasis of urban culture is on the leading edge, contemporary architecture is often the chosen mode of expression. Its crisp lines and planes can soothe as well as stimulate. But it's not the only way to go. A spacious, wood-paneled study might be the perfect restorative for someone who spends the day packed into a sterile corporate cubicle or in a so-hip-it-hurts workstation.

Intentionally contrasting styles in this way can work as an architectural antidote, having a rejuvenating effect on residents. However, in some cases—for instance, the converted electrical shop in Minneapolis (see p. 144) and the 18th-century town house in Philadelphia (see p. 194)—it's preferable to maintain a building's existing character. Indeed, preserving the status quo can, to varying degrees, be legislated by the city, particularly in situations involving structures that are designated historic landmarks.

Craftsmanship

Whether it's a showstopping element or a subtle touch of elegance, hand-worked materials and inventive details help blunt the sharp edges of city living. In a kitchen, a seamless expanse of exotic wood can delight the eye while it conceals pots, pans, and dishes. A narrow staircase threading upward through a space, its steel treads cantilevered in defiance of gravity, is as much art as it is architecture. A bathroom enclosure is imbued with a sense of serenity via a translucent-glass ceiling that sits atop walls and a floor that are completely covered in sea-green smalti tile; the effect is akin to being underwater. Such one-of-a-kind expressions reinforce the notion that in a place that seems to foster a heightened sense of anonymity, a special appreciation for beauty and craft also exists.

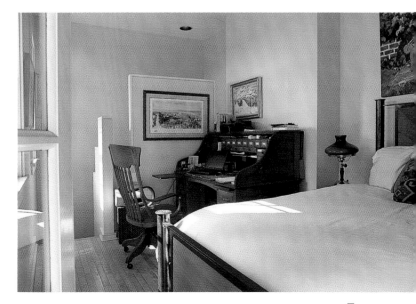

ABOVE Room for a garden is rare in city homes (particularly on upper floors), and even the most incidental opportunities are seized. This building's ample cornice makes a sturdy base for a window-box planting of herbs.

Nature

Although it's often a significant challenge to incorporate nature into the urban home, it's nonetheless a noble goal: When surrounded by shadowy towers of concrete, daylight and green spaces become priceless parts of the environment. (Realtors and developers, of course, have no trouble ascribing cash values to them, excelling at exaggerating assets such as a sliver of a "riv-vu" to ridiculous lengths.)

Terraces and balconies are the most common outdoor perches. They are rather tiny and, particularly at high floors, subject to winds that often curtail a full enjoyment of them. But that hardly discourages urbanites, who are nothing if not resourceful when faced with some extra square footage, no matter how vestigial it may be. A casual scan of the skyline exposes how many residents utilize them: as open-air closets for sports equipment and baby carriages, for example.

Landscaping opportunities become much more fertile at ground-floor and rooftop levels. Besides providing for genuine grass rather than AstroTurf underfoot, gardens extend living space in warmer months. Up on the roof, practical container plantings are favored for their relatively low maintenance and portability, which allow them

RIGHT In densely populated neighborhoods, fences enclosing ground-floor patios provide privacy while they enhance the sense of a natural refuge in the city.

When surrounded by shadowy towers of concrete, daylight and green spaces become priceless parts of the environment.

ABOVE Storage is most efficient when tailored not only to the objects being organized but also to the habits of the homeowner. In this dressing room, closely spaced, shallow, open shelves facilitate quick, unobstructed access.

to camouflage unsightly vent stacks and air-conditioning units.

Most city dwellers, though, must be content with a vicarious experience of the out-of-doors—that is, what can be seen from their windows. Creative techniques abound for bringing the view into focus. Where structurally feasible, interior walls can work in conjunction with windows, positioned so as not to obstruct sight lines, or openings can be cut into these walls to channel the vistas into adjacent rooms. Adroitly placed mirrors can effectively perpetrate an illusion—and on the cheap to boot.

Efficiency

The knee-jerk definition of "efficient design" when discussing city homes centers on ingenious storage tricks and clever solutions for problems unique to tight quarters. Most apartment occupants who own more than two pair of shoes will vouch for this. Built-in specialized storage (think sock cubbies) wastes the least amount of room but isn't always practicable. Fundamental to maximizing both custom and generic arrangements are a thorough, tape-measure-based tally of the articles to be stowed and an analysis of how frequently they're used.

On a broader level, efficiency means a logical organization of living space that responds both to occupants' needs and to existing architectural conditions. Large homes, as well as small ones, need to be planned well to function well. Convenient proximities have to exist between bedrooms and bathrooms and between the kitchen and dining areas. Circulation spaces such as hallways, foyers, and stairwells must be strategically laid out so they intrude minimally on living spaces yet efficiently link them together.

THE VARIETY OF CITY HOMES

City homes can be sorted into a few broad categories, each with its own inherent possibilities and problems. An overview of these attributes can help sort out what kind of home might be the best match for established and recent urbanites alike.

ABOVE AND BELOW Natural light is high on the list of urban-home assets. The design of this Baltimore residence (above) sacrificed square footage for sunlight in the location of a window wall on the side of the building, while in a town house in Chicago (below) a central atrium brightens the core of each floor.

Lofts

Currently charting the highest chic quotient—a critical factor in the status-conscious city—are lofts. They're characterized by 15-ft.-plus ceilings, expansive open bays marked by grids of columns, and floor-to-ceiling windows. Originally spaces scavenged out of warehouses and industrial buildings by artists in search of affordable living and working quarters, lofts have undergone a 180-degree turnaround. The raw quality that initially attracted the creative lot has been honed to a high polish, as a new, well-heeled class of inhabitants makes the loft a prominent stage for architectural experimentation. Some people revel in the unbounded space that lofts offer; others find them a bit too empty for comfort and prefer to divide them into smaller-scale zones. Walls that slide on tracks, platform floors, and pivoting panels are some of the devices used to reapportion the space while maintaining its flexible nature.

The open plan of the loft (not to mention its bohemian cachet) has been co-opted by real-estate developers, who now erect structures with interiors embellished with ersatz industrial character: exposed ductwork, raw concrete floors, faux brick walls, and non-structural columns. Where the resemblance falls shy of the original is, not surprisingly, in the living area. Many of these lofts-come-lately are only marginally larger than proportionately sized apartments; eliminating interior walls without expanding the perimeter only yields an average of 50 sq. ft. of "extra" space, little more than a generous closet.

Town houses, brownstones, and row houses

Town houses and their vernacular brethren—variously labeled brownstones and row houses in different parts of the country—evoke a domestic spirit that's opposite to the outré ambiance of the loft. They're all about structure: floor plans with familiar elements of BR, LR w/WBFP, DR, and K spread over several levels. Not infrequently, the layout needs updating to accommodate contemporary needs. Awkward strings of undersize chambers once used to house butlers and maids can be opened up to one another to create a home theater. Town houses are also ripe for more ambitious renovations, such as remaking the dark, enclosed core of the building into an atrium.

With opportunities for exterior expression so limited in the city,
town-house facades present a tempting canvas. If building code and
budget allow, you can make a permanent—and public—mark on the
town. Infill construction, where a vacant lot is developed from the
ground up, also poses the challenge of contributing to the local
streetscape. The buildings in a city put the past on display simultaneously with the present, the old with the new, in a physical reflection
of the advances of a culture over time.

Apartments

High-rises are the abode most emblematic of modern metropolitan
living. From bland brick cubes to Art Deco ziggurats to glittering
towers of plate glass and polished steel, these sky-high homes often
feature uninspired, cookie-cutter floor plans. Breaking out of these
boxes requires a purely urban brand of land-grab—one that's part
pragmatism, part conspicuous consumption: Buy an adjacent apartment and combine the two units.

Interior architecture has been likened to building a ship in a bottle, except that the inside of a bottle is free of elevator shafts, miles of ductwork, and colonies of rodents.

In larger cities especially, this annexation is becoming more commonplace as families opt to stay in town to rear their kids rather than retire to the suburbs. Given such motivated buyers, negotiations tend to favor the seller; neighbors can ask—and usually get—more than market value for their homes. And while some building-management boards take a dim view of combining apartments in this way, others believe that the resulting unique units contribute to the appeal of the property.

If the need to expand isn't quite so urgent, there are other, less Machiavellian methods to "grow" an apartment. Building a loft for sleeping and storage can often be managed, freeing up space for a compact home office. Removing selected walls, while more a reallocation of space than it is a substantial increase of it, can relieve a host of cramped conditions and help a small apartment live large.

BELOW The fractured floor plans typical of apartments can be softened by enlarging doorways and dissolving walls. Swinging panels of frosted glass accomplish this in a Chicago high-rise.

Studios and floor-through flats

Two ubiquitous subsets of the apartment genre deserve mention: studios and floor-through flats. Studios are for those who like their lives—and their possessions—orderly. Their snug quarters act as a spatial security blanket against the imposing scale of the city. Storage, always a dear commodity, is most precious to studio dwellers, and it is within their close-set walls that the artistry of the built-in reaches its zenith. Space-saving pocket doors, drop-down counters, Murphy beds—all stretch the capacity of these little rooms, which are frequently augmented by oddly shaped alcoves.

Here is also where multipurpose furnishings and fittings shine. Convertible sofas are the least of it. A veritable world of folding, telescoping, swiveling, nesting, collapsing, and chameleonic items do double duty in the cause of conserving inches. Chairs unfold into

LEFT Built-ins are not only the most efficient answer to storage problems but also open up the maximum amount of living area by minimizing the need for freestanding furnishings.

stepladders, coffee tables grow upward to become dining tables, and ottomans open to hold what-have-you.

Essentially a horizontal slice of a town house, floor-through flats typically have more charm than high-rises. The atmosphere they engender—parlor fireplaces with carved soapstone mantels, hardwood floors, and vintage bathroom fixtures—is of a gentler time. The flip side to this is that in their unimproved state, they lack the amenities of modern construction, such as central air conditioning, thermal windows, and elevator access. In addition to sharing an entry door, flats are sometimes connected by a common tenant stairway, which if it runs through a neighbor's apartment may prove problematic when remodeling.

Beyond these archetypal homes, there's a trove of unusual residential variants embroidering the urban fabric. It takes a singular vision to spot their domestic promise. Consider the architectural oxymoron of the skylit basement, a characteristic of 19th-century buildings in which the cellar extends out under a sidewalk that's made of glass block or tiles. Cursed with a subterranean site but blessed with loft-scale dimensions, it's not everyone's idea of an ideal home. There's the refurbished carriage house, its original hayloft transformed into a sleeping nook and the tack room turned into a galley kitchen. On a larger scale, living spaces can be carved out of erstwhile factories, offices, churches, or other recycled structures. Such is the case with the unlikely morphing of a former auto shop in Richmond, Virginia (see p. 54). And in an imaginative move to qualify for preservation tax incentives on his conversion of a high school into habitats, one New Orleans architect retained a few rows of audi-

BELOW One-room accommodations especially benefit from space-conscious fittings, like the tried-and-true Murphy bed. A folding screen conceals this one during daylight hours.

RIGHT The public role played by residences can't be ignored. A simple, restrained but colorful paint scheme can alleviate the monotony of blocks of repetitive exteriors, making a positive contribution to the streetscape.

BELOW City homes need to be a comfortable fit for their inhabitants. Sliding panels can regulate the wide-open spaces of lofts as desired, closing off areas when a more intimate atmosphere is wanted.

torium seating as well as chalkboards on the walls of many of the apartments.

MEETING THE CHALLENGE

Whether you opt to keep the architectural quirks or to smooth a space into a more customized environment, making a home in the city can be tricky. With the exception of town houses, it's an inside job in the strictest sense of the word—there's no backyard into which to build out or screened porch to box in; you're typically working within a fixed set of boundaries. Architects with city commissions find themselves configuring cabinetry and hashing out tile patterns instead of finessing rooflines and window details. But that doesn't mean projects are immune to complications; as with any construction endeavor, things can go awry.

The potential problems begin with the structure itself. Urban buildings are subject to more stresses than their suburban counterparts. Outside, they're exposed to concentrated quantities of pollutants; inside, their aging structural and mechanical systems have endured use by hundreds, if not thousands, of people over the years. These can range from annoying consequences of extended wear-and-tear—such as '70s-era parquet floor tiles that have shrunken away—to major headaches like corroded plumbing that afflicts an entire building.

TAILORING YOUR CITY HOME

Remodeling (and, obviously, building from scratch) is the chance to correct the mistakes of the past and tailor your home to your needs and taste. Make your priorities clear to yourself and everyone else and identify areas where you're willing to be flexible, so when the inevitable call for com-

promises arises, you won't have to whittle away at the parts of the design that matter most to you.

Whether it's reassigning a bedroom across the hall in order to catch the eastern light of the sunrise, integrating a home-computer network into an Edison-era electrical system, or turning a closet

into a sauna, a thoughtful review of your living habits is necessary before your domicile can be fine-tuned. This is especially true in work-at-home situations, where technology and aesthetics must be in sync.

RIGHT One way to defy the confines of a simple, boxlike volume is to set up unexpected views throughout the space. An open plan provides a great variety of vantage points from which to do just this; here, the glass-enclosed stair takes this idea a step further, facilitating oblique views between floors.

The thicket of red tape that surrounds construction in the city is another necessary nuisance. It can be of the municipal variety—the lengthy series of permits and reviews required by city officials—or the more informal but no less formidable codes of conduct adopted by building management. In trying to satisfy both worlds, it's possible to find yourself leading a weird kind of double life. On one hand, you're a vocal apologist to the neighbors for the dumpster that's occupying a prime parking slot while your demolition is underway; on the other, you're a righteous defender of your building-department-given right to renovate, no matter who it may upset.

Residential interior architecture has been likened to building a ship in a bottle, and, except that the inside of a bottle is free of elevator shafts, miles of ductwork, and colonies of rodents, it's an apt comparison. These hidden obstacles are just half of the picture, however. Neatly stashing a full complement of power tools, lumber, plas-

LEFT In this New York loft, the spread of light and the flow of space are both advanced by using a frosted glass panel as a door.

OPPOSITE This erstwhile auto shop in Richmond, Virginia, provides two coveted attributes for the city dweller: light and space. A second floor hugs a section of the perimeter of the building, housing bedrooms and a home office.

tering supplies, paint buckets, and drywall in the confines of a two-bedroom apartment in an unobtrusive yet accessible fashion takes the legerdemain of a magician and the discipline of a marine.

ABOVE Selectively retaining a structure's original proportions in a remodeling—as with this New Orleans town house—ties the house to its history and provides a solid base for new design work.

Similar hurdles exist on the logistical front. Orchestrating deliveries that range from a 500-lb. pallet of limestone pavers to lunch for the crew can push even the most organized person to the limit. (Wise homeowners will budget in a hefty gratuity for the doorman's troubles during the project, as well as a slush fund to cover the contractor's parking tickets.) At the other end of the job, a mix of diplomacy and wiles will stand you in good stead when it's time to clear six rooms of debris using just one union-operated service elevator.

Fortunately, you won't go through these dusty, noisy, nerve-wracking months of renovation alone. The urban talent pool of design professionals is a deep one. Architects are attuned to the aesthetics of the city, adept at evaluating existing conditions, and experienced in managing the byzantine construction process. There's a veritable guild of tradespeople and artisans for hire. Looking for a Venetian plaster pro? No problem. You'll find woodworkers and cabinetmakers with credits from decorative-arts departments of major museums on their resumes, and painters with similar pedigrees. For that finishing touch, call on an interior designer for guidance in navigating the myriad fabric and furnishings showrooms in the design district. Always get referrals and check references to seek out the truly qualified persons—this being the big, bad city, there are incompetent rip-off artists muddying the above-mentioned pool.

In the latest renaissance of the metropolis—this one so closely tied to the much-vaunted paradigm shift triggered by technological progress—a finely crafted home, as a place where the influence of the human hand and mind counters the uniformity of the everyday, may be more important than ever before. The trick is to tap into the energy and diversity of the city while balancing it with the sanctuary-like role an urban home needs to play. All the residences shown in these pages illustrate creative architectural connections between people and places, the past and the present—confirming that surviving the city of today can be accomplished with style and substance.

lofts

ALLEY ARCHITECTURE

DESIGN CHALLENGE > *to main-tain a sense of separation between working and living spaces in a narrow building*

OPPOSITE Eight skylights and a large southwest-facing window work together to balance the light sources in this top-floor photography studio. Floating a mezzanine office over the space preserves the open staging area and contains the filing and record-keeping functions.

In recent years, San Francisco has been a victim of its own prosperity and popularity, as the site of a dire housing shortage in which the city's residential vacancy rate has been measured in decimal points. When times are flush, the urban real-estate market goes into over-drive. Fueled by demand, all parties—buyers, sellers, and builders—are more receptive to unorthodox housing opportunities. Neighbor-hoods that had been quietly evolving at their own pace are suddenly on development steroids, for better or worse. There's no longer any right or wrong side of the tracks in terms of the relative desirability of certain parts of town.

A HOUSE BUILT
ON LAND OUT OF WATER

A telling example of this trend puts natural and unnatural geography on equal footing; in other words, artificially produced landforms are now as valuable as unadulterated ones when it comes to building sites. In a city renowned for its photogenic hills sprouting colorful Victorian town houses, the flatlands—a great deal of them landfill from leveling erstwhile hills or dredging the harbor—are increasingly pressed into service. Such is the case with Madeleine and Thomas's home, designed by Tanner Leddy Maytum Stacy Architects, which sits on earth where water used to be; it was recovered from the bay

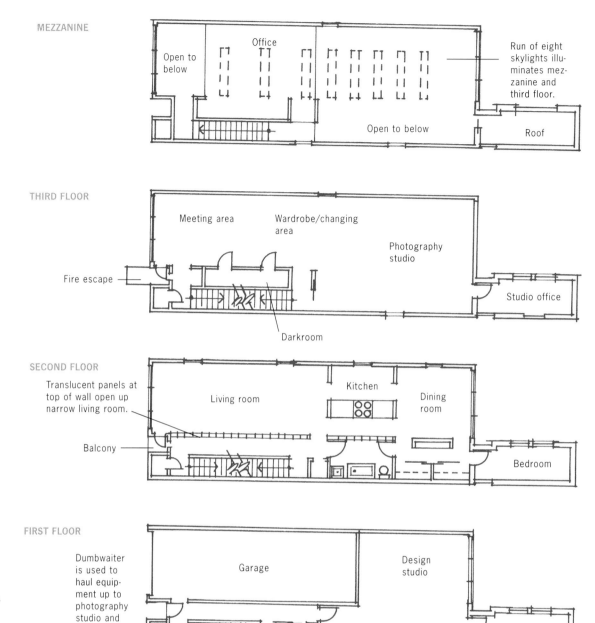

MEZZANINE

Office

Open to below

Run of eight skylights illuminates mezzanine and third floor.

Open to below

Roof

THIRD FLOOR

Meeting area

Wardrobe/changing area

Photography studio

Fire escape

Studio office

Darkroom

SECOND FLOOR

Translucent panels at top of wall open up narrow living room.

Living room

Kitchen

Dining room

Balcony

Bedroom

FIRST FLOOR

Dumbwaiter is used to haul equipment up to photography studio and mezzanine.

Garage

Design studio

BELOW In a residential real-estate crunch, the back streets of a city are no longer the sole domain of bike messengers and cabbies seeking shortcuts. In San Francisco, alley architecture has emerged as a vibrant alternative to the apartments and town houses of the city's well-populated hills, waterfront, and boulevards.

around the time of another land rush, circa 1849. Not only did this amphibious origin have an impact on the way the house was engineered, but interestingly it in turn also affected the building's appearance, beginning with its foundation and the structural framework.

Three pairs of concrete piers were sunk 40 ft. into the sandy soil. At ground level, they support a floating concrete slab. Growing upward from this at either end of the building are a couple of steel frames resembling stepladders, albeit ones with only three rungs. These act to stiffen the structure against earthquake forces and also allow the building to have an open, unobstructed floor plan.

WORKING ON TWO FLOORS

The resulting loft layout fulfills the homeowners' personal and professional needs. A creative couple—she's a graphic designer, he's a photographer who specializes in portrait and fashion shoots—they each required their own workspaces in the building. Her atelier is on the ground floor, behind the parking garage and adjacent to the rear garden. His photography studio occupies the top floor and mezzanine of the four-story structure, where it benefits from the light admitted by a series of eight slender, rectangular skylights running down the center of the 16-ft.-tall ceiling. A darkroom and wardrobe/changing area are on the main level, as well as a conference table.

The day-to-day desk jobs involved in running the studio—tasks utilizing computers, files, and the library—are concentrated on the mezzanine, which is suspended over the main staging space. In addi-

ABOVE Workspaces that have less specialized physical requirements can be incorporated into the floor plan with greater freedom. On the ground level, the design studio is set behind the garage enclosure. Camouflaging that barren wall and concealing a storage area are movable panels of magnetic white board and wood.

ABOVE AND LEFT In space-squeezed cities, it's the exceptional live/work scenario that gets the chance to be built from the ground up; most are remodeling projects, subject to the limitations of existing structures. The photography studio on the top floor of this new home was tailor-made to its user's requirements, with its spacious, well-lit staging area, darkroom facilities, and a mezzanine office.

tion to keeping office functions separate from creative ones, this arrangement makes it easy for people in the two spaces to communicate; everyone is within eye- and earshot. To spare the inconvenience of hauling equipment and supplies up and down, a dumbwaiter was installed just inside the entrance to the house, at the foot of the stairs. Each one of the floors has access to it. Seen from the street, the lift is enclosed in a shimmering, galvanized sheet-metal tower all its own, standing slightly apart from the bulk of the building and its glazed-grid facade (see the photo on p. 24).

LIVING IN BETWEEN

The living areas are located in the middle of the stack of stories, on the second floor. As in the rest of the structure, modest materials assembled with care and imagination elevate the rough-and-ready aesthetic to the artistic. Floors, as well as the occasional wall, are

LEFT Swinging doors take up precious space and solid doors block light—two things you don't want to do in an urban residence. This see-through, rolling door stylishly sidesteps these problems while simultaneously accomplishing its principal task: delineating rooms (the kitchen and the dining room) from one another.

BELOW Even if the commute is only a flight of stairs, it's important to maintain a sense of separation between working and living spaces. Compared to the raw quality of the studios, a distinctly domestic atmosphere reigns on the second floor of this home, where the living, sleeping, cooking, and dining activities are centered.

wood. While the ceilings on the other levels feature exposed joists and framing that are more compatible with a studio space, here, drywall overhead enhances the homey impression. Expanses of windows at both ends of the floor keep the space bright, helped by acrylic transoms that top the interior walls. The spread of light through the panels also counters the narrowness of the building.

In its organization and ambition, the quarters could hardly be simpler. The stair empties into the space at the point where the living area and the kitchen come together. The large living room overlooks the street, linked to a corridor of a kitchen that connects to a dining room. The bedroom is tucked away at the back of the house. Because the residential areas are confined to the second floor, visitors don't have to pass through (or intrude upon) the work areas,

INTERIOR DOORS

Even die-hard fans of open plans agree that there's a need for at least one interior door in a home. While the standard side-hinge model may adequately suit your purposes, there are several other types that, depending on the particular situation, may work as well or even better.

Pocket doors are the consummate conservers of space. They slide inside a wall cavity, disappearing completely when open. They're ideal for use in a blind corner or any place that's short on door-swing clearance. While typically installed as a single door, they can be effective when used in pairs, as in the parlors of turn-of-the-century brownstones. Pocket doors are at home in any environment, from traditional town houses to the most modern of living spaces.

Hanging track doors can be thought of as pocket doors turned inside out: They roll open and closed while suspended parallel to

Expanses of windows at both ends of the floor keep the space bright, helped by acrylic transoms that top the interior walls.

preserving the distinction between the two types of space.

While its comparably small size keeps the structure from being mistaken for any of the warehouse facilities or light-industry buildings that characterize much of the environs, its exterior is heavily influenced by them. The steel stepladder frame is visible on the outside of the building, defining its edges and the various floor levels. Over an innocuous garage door, a column of operable awning windows rises up through a field of fixed-glass panes. The result—a loose, casual combination of industrial and international styles—adds an unexpected bit of architectural sophistication to the texture of the alley.

ABOVE There's no underestimating the need for an additional degree of retreat from life in the city. In a relief from the large-scale, open studio, this small office provides a quiet, private space for reading or reflection.

OPPOSITE Light can be a powerful tool in transforming space. In this home, translucent panels at the top of select interior walls are an effective way to offset the living room's extreme narrowness.

the surface of a wall. Like pocket doors, they can be made of virtually any material. For lightweight partitions, the tracks can be mounted on the ceiling; large or heavy panels that need more stabilizing run on tracks that are attached high up on

the wall. Because they operate "outside" the wall, the doors can be fitted with shelves on one side, providing extra storage and display areas.

Pivot doors swing around a point midway along the width of the door, rather than along its edge. The swing radius varies, depending on the size of the door. When closed, there's no telltale hardware visible; the act of opening it—one pushes on a blank section of wall, to have it unexpectedly give way and reveal a hidden

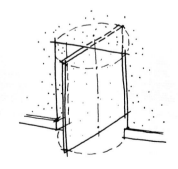

space beyond—is an abstract, dramatic action. Pivot doors add a sculptural, architectural element to a home.

SEVEN ARCHES DEFINE A TRIBECA LOFT

DESIGN CHALLENGE > *to gracefully and purposefully integrate a central bearing wall into the floor plan*

OPPOSITE The proverbial immovable object—in this case, a centrally located brick load-bearing wall— always presents a design challenge. The arched parti- tion was previously walled over and painted white; in the current scheme, which puts a diversity of textures and materials firmly at the fore, it's fully exposed.

The upturn in large-scale residential construction has altered the look of the city in ways that are more often expedient than they are aesthetic. It's an exceptional new apartment tower that contributes an improvement to the skyline or to the streetscape; when its con- struction demands the destruction of smaller buildings, the loss is often compounded. Even when the exteriors of low-rise buildings are maintained or restored as part of a conversion to housing units, the interiors are frequently eviscerated and diced into generic, drywalled habitats.

So it's an especially heartening surprise to encounter a piece of authentic urban archaeology upon entering Debbie and Polar's loft, located in the TriBeCa neighborhood of New York City, whose former commercial storerooms and showrooms are rapidly being turned into homes. Anchoring the physical floor plan as well as the concep- tual structure of the loft is an original architectural feature from the turn of the century: A brick bearing wall, pierced by seven plain but graceful arches, runs right down the middle of the loft. It's not treated by Dean/Wolf Architects as a precious artifact or decorative element, though; it is, rather, the linchpin of a thoroughly contemporary design.

Anchoring the physical floor plan as well as the conceptual structure of the loft is an original architectural feature from the turn of the century: a brick-bearing wall, pierced with seven plain but graceful arches.

ABOVE Outside, the building shows no signs of the renovation within, preserving the character of the block.

IT'S ALL ABOUT THE WALL

One of the normal purposes of a wall is to divide and separate, but this one is different. It acts more like a seam, its arches providing the framework for knitting together not only spaces but also various functions and materials. There are two strands of activities woven through its openings: living and working.

The eastern half of the third-floor loft is given over to the couple's studios, which are placed to the right and left of the entrance to the home. Oversize steel and fiberglass doors can close off the studios individually or in combination, away from the living spaces.

Polar's musical pursuits are spread over two areas. In addition to a large workroom, there's a soundproof composing chamber,

RIGHT In this loft, the central wall works as a corridor would in an apartment: It organizes a sequence of spaces. The couple's studios are on one side, their living quarters on the other.

which, in the metropolitan equivalent of the good fences/good neighbors maxim, has been aurally isolated with layers of neoprene and concrete.

At the other end of the loft, Debbie's drawing studio features a built-in table (one of several throughout the space) that's used to show off the pair's numerous personal mementos and articles of artistic inspiration. The display pedestals are complemented by a battery of storage closets and shelving. By placing objects of memory, expression, and play along the wall, the lines between creative work and creative play begin to break down throughout the space.

Sliding panels of Homasote, a structural fiberboard that's made entirely of recycled newsprint, line the brick partition in the drawing studio. Debbie uses them for tacking up sketches and papers. The panels cover the arch that opens through to the master bedroom.

ABOVE Storage can be configured to conceal or reveal, and there's a sensible and generous mixture of both types in this loft. Closets line many of the walls, while platforms and tables for displaying various collections are prominent elements of the interior architecture.

ABOVE AND RIGHT For a family where the parents work at home, an open floor plan may not provide the privacy they need to conduct their businesses in peace. Here, fiberglass panels the size of walls can swing shut as desired, producing a variety of spatial configurations. One closes off the child's play area from the living room (above) another shields the music studio (right).

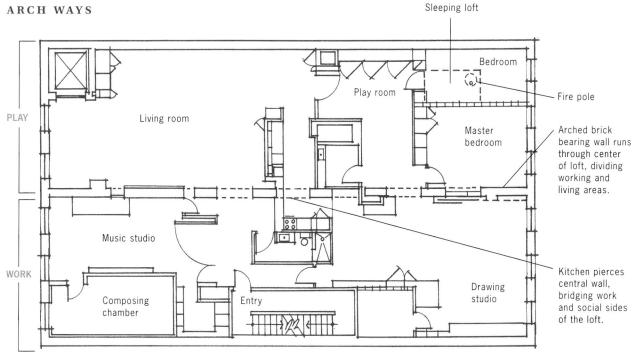

Sleeping loft

Bedroom

Play room

Living room

Master bedroom

Fire pole

Arched brick bearing wall runs through center of loft, dividing working and living areas.

PLAY

WORK

Music studio

Composing chamber

Entry

Drawing studio

Kitchen pierces central wall, bridging work and social sides of the loft.

A CHANGE OF MATERIALS ON THE FAMILY SIDE

This point of the wall also signals a switch in the palette of building materials used in the home. Instead of fiberglass and steel, the family sections of the loft—the bathrooms, kitchen, and bedroom enclosures—are characterized by compositions in plywood and Plycem, a lightweight portland-cement panel that is noncombustible and is treated with silicone to make it water-resistant. With its smooth, matte surface and fine grain, it bears a convincing resemblance to limestone. The neutral colors of these materials, lighter and warmer than the gunmetal tones found in the working half of the loft, are more befitting a residential setting.

But that's not to say the loft has been wholly domesticated; a sense of creativity is still present in the living areas. In the child's bedroom, for instance, a fire pole at the corner of the sleeping loft sets the stage for all sorts of imaginative games, not to mention making getting up in the morning anything but mundane. Adjacent to the room, an open play area infuses this portion of the home with a feeling of fun.

The kitchen sits in the center of the floor. Perhaps because cooking (particularly in an open kitchen) can be as much theater as housekeeping chore, it's the only "room" to actually pierce the brick wall, bridging both work and social sides of the space. A counter, which houses prep and clean-up functions, extends into the living/dining area; passing through an arch and turning 90 degrees, it becomes home to the refrigerator and range.

ABOVE A bold yet resourceful way of maximizing light in a windowless room is to use a translucent material for its walls. This bath is enclosed by steel and fiberglass panels that are suspended from the ceiling, allowing a band of mysterious, greenish light to emanate from the base when the lights are low.

NEW YORK CITY

ABOVE AND LEFT With cooking becoming more synonymous with entertainment, kitchens are increasingly designed as communal spaces, especially in loft settings. The brick bearing wall and the kitchen intersect in the heart of the home, with the kitchen's main counter lacing through one of the arches to connect the living and working halves of the loft, continuing the weaving concept.

HOME OFFICES

The home office: epicenter of organization—or it should be. Whether you're a full-time home-based businessperson or a homeowner just looking to carve out some space for bill paying, the importance of an orderly work environment can't be underestimated. Without being obsessive about it, a considered arrangement of space, furnishings, and equipment that keeps the most frequently used items within a 30-in. radius will help lessen the daily grind.

The physical setup of your home will determine if your office can be completely separated from your living space or if it will have to somehow share the same square footage. With wireless technologies coming on strong, another angle on the issue emerges: Is a permanent workstation desirable or should you cut the cords and go mobile? In either case, try to keep a healthy distance between your living and work areas; the payoff is a preservation of visual and psychological integrity. If you lack a door between the two, a screen or curtain can help conceal and partition the areas.

LEFT While spaces
in this loft are
tied together by
brick arches,
steel doors pro-
vide a convincing
barrier where
necessary; here,
one separates
the music work-
room from the
rest of the home.

For both efficiency and ergonomic
purposes, an L-shaped or kidney-
contoured desk is optimal. With
these configurations, the contents of
the desk come to you, rather than
the other way around. A worktable
may be the pinnacle of minimal chic,
but you may eventually miss the convenient storage provided by drawers.
A stylish and functional compromise
is a taboret, a wheeled file cabinet.

Walls are an often-overlooked
organizational opportunity. Hanging
shelves can be a lifesaver, especially
in areas that are too awkward or
small to hold freestanding bookcases.
Shelves should be no higher than
20 in. above the desktop; otherwise,
they're beyond reach from a sitting
position. Cork boards and magnetic
strips are other quick-fix accessories
that can put vertical surfaces to work.

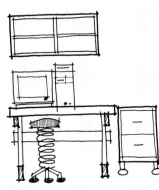

BRINGING A BOX TO LIFE

DESIGN CHALLENGE > *to endow the featureless shell of a loft with flexible, multipurpose spaces*

OPPOSITE A common symptom of loft conversions of newer buildings is a lack of architectural presence; blank walls abound. Inserting new walls can define spaces and add character. This brushed-aluminum wall reflects afternoon sun throughout the living area.

They started with a conspicuously empty concrete box: long, windowless side walls, a ceiling spanned by box beams, and a bare floor. The views of the Boston skyline, which are visible from each end of the room, were its most compelling visual component. Gary, the homeowner, asked Ruhl Walker Architects to effect a metamorphosis of this raw space into a multifunctional residential loft, while keeping the quality of the space fluid and unobstructed.

ANGLED, FREESTANDING WALLS
KEEP THE BOXY FEELING AT BAY

Given the owner's request, it could come as a surprise that the architects dropped more walls into the loft. But while a move like this might not seem in line with the objective of openness, these aren't ordinary walls. First of all, they're positioned so they don't chop up the space; they run alongside the perimeter walls at a slight angle, at some points standing several feet away from them. Adding that bit of extra dimension relieves the unbroken flatness of the wall planes and also curbs the corners of the 27-ft. by 65-ft. room, lessening its big-box feeling.

The new walls are made of two different materials—one is brushed aluminum, the other is hand-ground acrylic set into a steel framework—which, unlike cold concrete, inject a warmth and visual

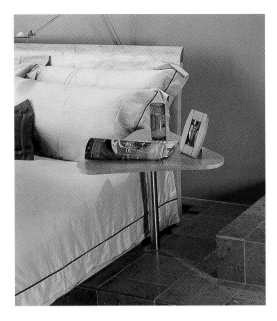

ABOVE Because they're integral to the architecture, built-ins are effective aesthetic reference points, keeping the interior design from heading off-track. Even a small element like this nightstand is an elegant reminder of the beauty brought by simple forms.

BELOW Like an industrial *shoji* screen, the translucent acrylic wall runs the length of the loft, diffusing morning light deep into the space.

Where walls usually block out light, these actually promote it.

texture into the loft. But they're more than simple surface effects. Where walls usually block out light, this pair actually promotes it. The translucent acrylic catches the morning light and wicks it into the heart of the space. Later in the day, as the sun crosses over to the other side of the loft, its rays hit the metal wall and bounce back through the living area.

Another unusual attribute of the walls is that some of them move. Slide one end of the aluminum wall toward the middle of the space a bit and the polygonal guest bedroom comes into sight. Extend the panels fully to the outer wall of the building and it's back under wraps. (This route through the living area, though, isn't the sole access to the visitor's suite; there's a doorway just inside the entrance to the loft that allows for private comings and goings.)

The master bedroom is set off from the rest of the loft by a straight stretch of bypass panels that slip surreptitiously into a slot in the side wall when not in use. When the 4-ft.-wide, 11-ft.-tall partitions are closed, they form an unambiguous boundary to the main living area—there's little chance of any partygoers accidentally wandering into this personal space.

LEFT Natural finishes and forms are a refreshing antidote to the harsh realities of urban living. In the master bath, the walls are honed limestone and marble tiles. The cabinetry is crafted of clear-figured maple.

ABOVE Windows at each end of the loft catch the light
twice a day, at sunrise and sunset.

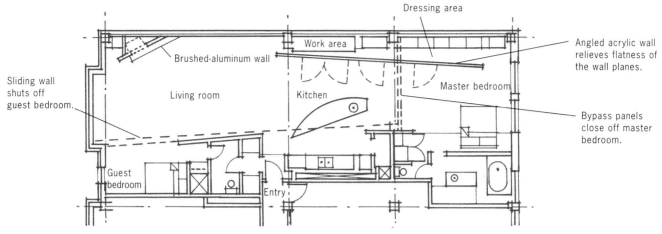

Dressing area

Work area

Angled acrylic wall
relieves flatness of
the wall planes.

Brushed-aluminum wall

Sliding wall
shuts off
guest bedroom.

Living room

Kitchen

Master bedroom

Bypass panels
close off master
bedroom.

Guest
bedroom

Entry

ABOVE The dressing area shares a window with the master bedroom, while it's simultaneously screened from the space by acrylic panels.

RIGHT Walls don't have to be visible to be viable. A quartet of 4-ft. by 11-ft. bypass doors can close off the bedroom from the rest of the loft and later slide into a pocket in the wall, out of sight.

WALLS SERVE AS DOORS AND VICE VERSA

Having finessed the open floor plan, the walls go on to form the basis of the other item on Gary's wish list: functional flexibility. It's an attribute that's indispensable to all one-room living situations, whether it's a cozy studio or spacious loft. Here, the acrylic panels provide covert cover for features that would otherwise intrude upon the space with an unruly assortment of wardrobe, office, and closet doors.

At the far end of the loft, the panels screen a walk-in closet/ dressing room from the master bedroom. Closer to the center of

the space, two of the panels swing outward to reveal a desk. Not opening them fully against the wall creates a sense of enclosure—providing a sometimes welcome opportunity for privacy while working. In a bonus that's sure to strike a chord with anyone who's ever done business out of the home, it's also possible to conceal the office at a moment's notice—an appealing alternative to scrambling to tidy it up.

Falling between the bedroom and the living area, the kitchen commands the middle of the floor in an exclamation of color and a concentration of materials: a bank of yellow aniline-dyed maple cabinets, a stainless-steel backsplash, and green granite counters. Such an animated density balances the lighter, airier ends of the loft. Adjacent to the entry, a large, bowfront island sits like a rock in a river, buffering the cooking area from foot traffic and directing visitors through the fluid space.

ABOVE Open-plan living can quickly dissolve into visual chaos without a cogent strategy to combat it. Complete with storage and filing systems, tack space, and task lighting, a compact work area sits behind hinged acrylic doors.

OPPOSITE The most prudent design strategy often reinforces, rather than resists, existing conditions. Based on the long expanse of windowless walls in this loft, a galley plan is the logical layout for the kitchen.

ABOVE Introducing contrast—of form, material, or scale—adds an interesting element of tension to a space. At one end of the loft, a curvaceous plywood chaise floats in a grid of red birch cabinets.

ABOVE The kitchen's colors and materials bring their own brightness to the midpoint of the loft. Aniline-dyed maple cabinets glow yellow; the stainless-steel backsplash gleams.

DOUBLE-DUTY FURNITURE

Just as spaces can serve multiple functions (as demonstrated by Gary's loft), so can furniture—and the myriad forms that pieces can assume are often a whimsical exercise in artistic alchemy. Particularly in smaller homes, double- or even triple-duty furnishings can help maximize living space. The good news is that there are plenty of ready-made designs on the market; they're not the exclusive domain of custom manufacturers and cabinetmakers.

What better way to develop chameleonic abilities than with one of the most space-hogging items in the house: the bed. The convertible sofa is, of course, a staple of modern apartment living, and for a long time was the only option for those seeking a dual-purpose bed. It offers a simple choice to its users: sit or sleep.

Now it's possible to mix and match functions to one's needs. Short on storage? Platform beds are fitted with drawers to handle an overflow of small items. Another design is hinged at the

base of the headboard, allowing the mattress to be lifted up, revealing a spacious, open compartment that is the same size as the bed.

If it's surface area that's lacking, a clever update of the foldaway Murphy bed may ease the crunch. When the bed is in its upright position, a panel can be pulled down from its underside, creating a table that can be used for dining or working. Another improvement over its predecessor is the fact that the unit is entirely self-supporting, so it can be located anywhere, without attaching it to the floor or wall. With a finished panel on the back, it can even act as a partition or room divider. It's available in twin, full, and queen sizes.

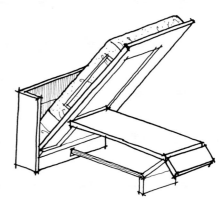

A SENSITIVE SEPARATION

DESIGN CHALLENGE > *to create a comfortable, productive live/work environment*

Working and living in the same space isn't always what it's cracked up to be. Sure, there's no commute to worry about and you can shuffle around your home office in fuzzy slippers and dressing gown, but there is a downside. The phone can ring well beyond business hours, the temptation to work all the time (or not at all) is omnipresent, and chronic cabin fever wars with the disquieting feeling of occupying a perpetually open house, with colleagues and clients constantly passing in and out. What could be called a "disciplined flexibility" in both habits and habitat is at the core of a comfortable, productive living/ working environment.

A WELL-ORDERED ATELIER

The central part of this 12th-floor loft is given over to homeowner Page Goolrick's architecture studio. It's simply appointed and laid out, with no-frills desks and drafting tables spaced widely apart, emphasizing the openness of the room. Low-slung filing cabinets edge the walls, and computer equipment—the aesthetic bane of most offices on the planet—is neatly placed in niches on the desk pedestals, with cords and wires corralled in pliable plastic conduit. Across the room from the window, bookcases loaded with supplies and documents capitalize on the 14-ft. height. In the studio and the other rooms, clear maple floors and white walls and ceilings bounce natural light through the space.

OPPOSITE Where public and private areas coexist, the architectural detailing must be disciplined. Meticulously clean lines—the absence of boxy wall cabinets, cooking paraphernalia, and bulky appliances—allow the kitchen to double as a conference room.

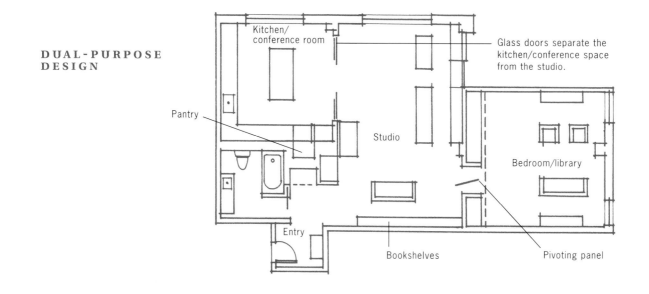

DUAL-PURPOSE DESIGN

Kitchen/conference room

Glass doors separate the kitchen/conference space from the studio.

Pantry

Studio

Bedroom/library

Entry

Bookshelves

Pivoting panel

ABOVE With picture windows, views are simultaneously part of the interior and the outdoors; the windows act as a framed photograph. In this kitchen, the view of the southern Manhattan skyline is very much a presence during meals or meetings.

There's no mistaking this room as a place that means business. But many live/work situations are porous, letting little things from domestic life infiltrate the work area: a television, a microwave oven, or a too-comfy chair. However well- (or un-) intentioned, such spillover has greater consequences than being unsightly or incongruous; it dilutes the sense of purpose assigned to a particular space. And that effect goes both ways. If the dining table has been taken over by office sprawl or the bedroom has been co-opted by a special business project, it's easy to lose sight of the sanctity of the home. Should it be absolutely necessary for personal and professional functions to overlap in a single location, it's got to be planned down to the last detail. This loft contains a terrific, albeit unlikely, example of a successful crossover space: The kitchen is also a conference room.

THE COVERT KITCHEN PLAYS A DOUBLE ROLE

Even under strictly residential circumstances, the kitchen—with its full complement of large and small appliances and diverse, specialized storage needs—can be problematic to design. When it comes to dealing with the kitchen in home/office combos, a common approach is to shrink it down and seal it off, essentially turning it into a closet with a stove and refrigerator. Such a move might be appropriate for a coffee-break room in a big, button-down firm, but this setting—as a casual, live/work environment—obviously has a

ABOVE Neatness counts in live/work scenarios. Subtly concealed behind translucent plastic-film doors and reached by a wheeled ladder, a bank of bookcases efficiently organizes documents and samples in the architect's studio.

different agenda. Goolrick decided to make a quiet showcase of the room while casting it in an ambiguous role. She separated the 20-ft. by 20-ft. space from the studio with a set of industrial but elegant glass doors.

Inside the room, base cabinets run along two walls and are topped by a stretch of brushed stainless steel. There's ample pin-up space and projection areas for presentations. A utility cart can be wheeled out from the counter and positioned where it's needed. Appliances are strictly of the under-counter variety—even the cooking hobs are hidden under hinged sections of steel. Only the arc of a polished chrome faucet breaks the horizontal plane. So seamless is the design that the space can be used for meetings with clients without compromising the professional atmosphere. All this, and the basic kitchen facilities—for cooking, cleaning, and storage— remain intact and undiminished.

ABOVE Looks can—and at times must—be deceiving when trying to keep up appearances. Because of its role as a meeting room, a lot of the storage this kitchen needs had to go undercover. A hidden pantry is located behind a counter-height cart that rolls out from the wall. Stainless-steel lids camouflage the cooktop.

A THICK WALL PROVIDES A BUFFER BETWEEN WORK AND LIVING SPACES

While the integration of two different functions was very much the point in the kitchen/conference-room area, the separation of functions was the prime objective when planning the private space of the loft. Because virtually every action, every day, is concentrated under one roof in live/work arrangements, an intense lifestyle is often the result. For that reason, having a buffer between these two worlds—one that offers not just a physical retreat but some psychological relief as well—is key. Put another way, it's important to be able to get away without having to go away. If you're dedicating the better part of your waking hours to running a home-based business, there had better be something more substantial than a hollow-core door marking the boundary between the living room and your livelihood.

Goolrick's solution creates a genuine sense of passage without squandering space with a conventional corridor. Breached by a pivoting panel, a 28-in.-thick wall divides the bedroom from the studio. Pushing open the door and walking through it, there's a palpable feeling of transition; once over the threshold, the ambience takes a distinct turn toward the personal. The windows are smaller and sport shades; the couch and armchairs offer soft, upholstered contours; and the room itself is more intimately proportioned. Even though the office is less than a yard away, the sense of separation is complete.

The wall literally has a practical side to it. In the bedroom, it provides a veritable mother lode of storage. Clothes closets, a television, and books rise to the ceiling; a rolling ladder, attached midway up the wall, puts the contents within reach. It's the final underscore to the significance of careful spatial planning on both a large and small scale in a multipurpose environment.

ABOVE "Making room" sometimes means tearing an existing room apart. As part of her campaign to reclaim every inch of usable space, Goolrick stripped off wallboard that disguised utility stacks but took up precious floor area. A partial second floor that sliced through the bedroom/library was also removed.

It's a tall order. Lacking a garage and famously short on storage for big items, city dwellers typically don't have the luxury of keeping a stepladder on the premises. How, then, to cope with overhead tasks like changing a ceiling fixture or replacing a book on the uppermost shelf of a 14-ft. wall? Here are some space-conscious ways to scale the heights.

Toekick step stool. Designed for those times when you just need a boost up to the top shelf of the kitchen cupboard, this device can be stowed under a bathroom vanity, bookcase, or wherever there's raised cabinetry. Talk about getting the most out of underutilized space: Folded flat, the stool slips into a section of

the cabinet plinth where it remains out of sight yet within easy reach.

Ship ladder. A generic label for an installation where rungs and grab rails are permanently attached to the wall in a strictly vertical path. Occupying no floor area to speak of, it's good for fixed, frequent access, like climbing up to a loft bed. But because it's not a hands-free ascent, ship

LEFT In one-room living, sleeping accommodations need to be inconspicuous. Shielded by a folding screen by day, that classic space conserver, the Murphy bed, puts in a nightly appearance in the bedroom.

BELOW In compact city quarters, a wall that merely divides space is either an indulgence or a wasted opportunity. This wall between the office and the bedroom is built out to 28 in. in order to contain books and clothing. As in the studio, a library ladder provides access to storage on the upper levels.

ladders aren't suitable for situations where you're carrying loads up or down. A variation for the very agile: frame foothold cavities into the wall.

Rolling ladder. There are two basic types of wheeled ladders. Freestanding models, similar to stairs, can be positioned anywhere they're needed. While they're sturdy, stabile, and add a sculptural note to a room, they also gobble up a lot of floor space. The other style of rolling ladder slides along an elevated rail or track that's bracketed to the wall. Standing parallel to the wall when not in use, it easily pulls out to a comfortable incline for climbing. Some models can be adapted to turn corners.

ON THE FRINGE OF THE CITY

DESIGN CHALLENGE > *to convert an industrial warehouse to living space on a site zoned for manufacturing use*

The *garage* is more than 600 sq. ft. To disbelieving metropolitans accustomed to entire residences topping out at that mark, the statement bears repeating (though perhaps that would be cruel). Suffice it to say that homeowners Margaret Moore and Jeffrey Levine (who is also the architect) don't lack for closet space.

The plusses of living on the fringe of the city—especially a smaller one like Richmond, with about 200,000 inhabitants—as opposed to in its center are noteworthy. Granted, there's no doorman or glitzy lobby, and there might not be a trendy boutique or club on the corner—yet. But the tradeoffs are more issues of substance than they are of style. It's relatively quiet and affordable. And of course, there's the glorious opportunity for space: in this case, nearly 4,000 habitable square feet of it.

RIGHT AND OPPOSITE Adaptive reuse may involve changing a building's appearance as well as its function. The once-blank face of this warehouse gets a new identity with the addition of a towering screen porch. The interior is simply rendered in concrete block, drywall, and metal.

ABOVE City living isn't limited to downtown districts. Opting to settle on the edge of a metropolitan area—note the nearness of the Richmond skyline—often means getting more home for less money.

INDUSTRIAL ORIGINS

From just about anywhere in their perch on Richmond's historic Church Hill, Margaret and Jeffrey enjoy a panoramic view of the city. It's a sight that probably wasn't appreciated by the previous owners of the building, who most recently used the 40-year-old structure as a mechanical-supply warehouse. The place was pretty banged up. The corrugated metal siding was dented and rusted out, and most of the insulation batting had disappeared, along with the linoleum floor tiles in the offices. A loading dock overflowed with trash. Still, the

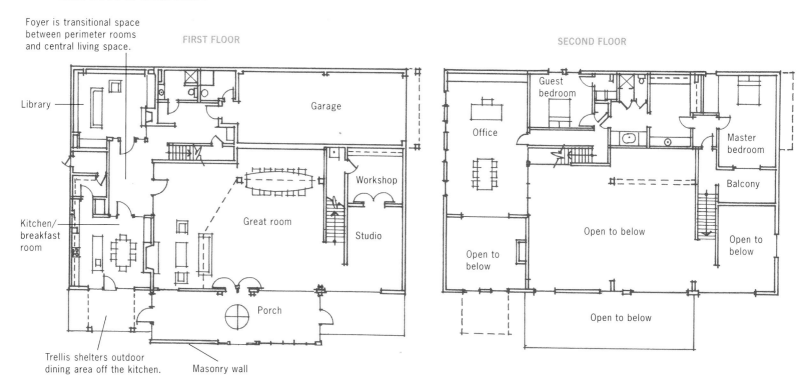

FIRST FLOOR

Foyer is transitional space between perimeter rooms and central living space.

Library

Kitchen/
breakfast
room

Garage

Workshop

Great room

Studio

Porch

Trellis shelters outdoor dining area off the kitchen.

Masonry wall

SECOND FLOOR

Guest bedroom

Office

Master bedroom

Balcony

Open to below

Open to below

Open to below

Open to below

---

hillside site and the roomy 50-ft. by 80-ft. size of the steel-framed structure held promise.

The couple spent about five years planning and refurbishing the property, a campaign that included obtaining a special-use permit that allowed them to construct a residence on a site that was zoned for manufacturing use. Once the project was approved, they seized the chance to create a home that was strictly for themselves, unencumbered by co-op board restrictions or concerns about what floor-plan design would yield the maximum return at resale.

FROM WAREHOUSE TO OUR HOUSE

Without straying far from its industrial origins, the facade was given a convincing makeover. Rising from a new concrete slab, a 25-ft.-tall steel-strut screened-porch structure fronts the building proper. As an overlay on what's essentially still a commercial edifice, it softens and centralizes its appearance. Half of the face of the porch is shielded by a masonry wall. It's a solid visual balance to the transparent screen and glass components and also provides strategic shade. A serious trellis stands to the side of the porch, where it shelters an outdoor dining area that sits off the kitchen. Much of the welding and assembly of the metal frames was done on-site, in the space that eventually became the main living area of the home.

The existing exterior walls of the building were refurbished where necessary, but the building's original footprint was maintained as part of the adaptation. The ground floor is divided into two parts. Running along the rear and side of the building is a chain of discrete

ABOVE Climate control is an issue to be reckoned with, as residents of large, lofty spaces can attest. In hot weather or cold, ceiling fans keep air from stratifying and can be synchronized with strip heaters to boost temperatures. A Rumford fireplace warms up the seating area in the far corner of this room.

ABOVE Continuing material usage or motifs helps integrate new work with old. The screened-porch addition expounds on the original metal structure while expanding the home's usable space.

rooms; enclosed by walls, they're easier to heat and cool than large, open areas. The interior walls of several of these spaces are glass, so light from the large openings on the front of the house can penetrate into the rooms. The kitchen, library, utility, and storage rooms are connected to one another by a foyer, which serves as a transition area to the central living space. Certainly by normal city standards, it is vast, measuring 40 ft. by 32 ft. with a seemingly sky-high ceiling of 20 ft. The truck-size openings where a pair of overhead doors had originally been situated have been glazed, producing a mammoth window wall.

The voluminous space easily accommodates a second level, where two bedrooms, a bath, laundry facilities, and a spacious office are located along the back and sides of the building. A pair of staircases have been added to the plan. While the spaces upstairs are con-

ABOVE Large volumes often need a bit of toning down. To mitigate any cavernous feelings, a freestanding partition at one end of the living area is kept to a height of 9 ft. That detail is echoed on the opposite wall by a band of masonry.

LEFT Ways to capitalize on vertical space vary according to the environment. Looking up reveals many opportunities for expansion, from carving out full-height bookcases in an apartment to dropping in an entire upper floor, as done here.

BORN-AGAIN BUILDINGS

As the urban-housing market becomes increasingly competitive (in some locations, that's already a euphemism for "impossible"), there's a renewed interest in creative responses to this demand. Once the domain of starving artists and social activists, urban housing is today attracting influential real-estate developers.

Adaptive reuse—where a building or facility not originally intended to be used as a resi-

dence is legally converted to one—continues to appeal to adventurous types. Still, it's sage advice to shed any romantic notions about playing the urban pioneer; these projects can be exhaustive undertakings. Those who proceed must be patient, persistent, detail-oriented, and (as they say at the brokerage) comfortable with risk.

Just knowing where the lot lines are isn't enough. Be pre-

pared to provide information on the past, present, and future of the property with regard to a wide range of issues. Zoning history can be a make-or-break factor. Estimates on how the new residence will affect traffic flow and congestion will be examined. Some municipalities are particularly concerned with tangible benefits to the surrounding community (for example, will there be any landscaping improvements

The existing exterior walls of the building were refurbished where necessary, but the building's original footprint was maintained as part of the adaptation.

tiguous, it's more direct to use one set of stairs to reach the office and the other for the master suite at the opposite end of the floor. New windows were selectively punched into the exterior walls for views and ventilation.

The materials used in the project—corrugated metal for the roof, masonry block on select interior walls, steel framing, and concrete flooring—all work to emphasize the commercial character of the building. It was important to Jeffrey and Margaret that the design of the home "remember" its origins.

While the architecture has maintained its strong aesthetic ties to the industrial, the landscape has taken a fully different turn. A garden of drought-tolerant ornamental grasses and plants native to the region was planted around a series of focal points in a pastoral counterpoint to the concrete jungle that rises at the foot of Church Hill.

ABOVE It's not only buildings that can be reinvented, so can the landscape. Reclaimed from hardpan, the garden—comprised of hardy, low-maintenance plants—is well suited to demanding urban conditions.

that would be appreciated by the general public or exterior lighting upgrades that would deter street crime?). Can—or must—the building be made compliant with current energy standards? Are there any historic-preservation requirements that need to be met? These are just a few of the areas that must be addressed and resolved.

Once the plans pass muster, construction—and all its attendant

surprises—may begin. You may find a buried oil tank not noted on the original blueprints or electrical wiring dating from the gaslight era. By anticipating encounters with obstacles like these (and by budgeting accordingly for the extra time and

cash needed to deal properly with them), you won't be completely derailed when they occur.

What's the payoff? As with Jeffrey and Margaret, a one-of-a-kind home in a city where "one size fits all" is the status quo is its own reward.

A CHORUS OF MATERIALS

DESIGN CHALLENGE > *to incorporate a fresh mix of materials and finishes to enliven a basic, boxlike loft*

OPPOSITE In older buildings, original details in good condition are always worth keeping. Here, an expanse of double-hung wood windows is the focal point of the living room and frames a backdrop of arches across the street.

In most cities, there's an unofficial attribute to every address that transcends the zip code. San Francisco's Haight Ashbury conjures images of psychedelically painted Victorians, staid town houses populate the Back Bay section of Boston, and the Garden District in New Orleans is known for its gracious Georgian mansions. New York City, of course, has no shortage of these iconic addresses, from the resurgent Striver's Row brownstones to the white-glove apartment buildings of Park Avenue. But more compelling than the travelogue images are the door-to-door details—the all-night newsstand, the mom-and-pop laundromat, the corner sandwich shop—that give an area its true character.

Bookstores, cinemas, and a farmer's market provide a cultural context for the home featured here, a 1,400-sq.-ft. loft on a side street in a bustling New York City neighborhood. Marble Fairbanks Architects developed a plan for the ninth-floor space that mirrors this creative milieu. One way the firm did so is by incorporating a fresh mix of materials and finishes into the design. Slate, steel, translucent glass, and slender cylinders of clear acrylic—all in tempered amounts to avoid sensory overload—are combined to add interest to otherwise ordinary surfaces. Another tactic plays with perspective by changing floor levels. When seen from different heights

RIGHT Varying surface treatments is one way to define different spaces in an open plan. From the entryway, you can take in many of the materials that give this loft its visual texture. Cork tiles, clear acrylic rods, and translucent glass add interest to a generously scaled but otherwise basic box.

BELOW Using something other than a stock 3/0 door to close off rooms opens the gate to creativity. When not in use, this guest suite can disappear behind rolling panels of aniline-dyed Finn plywood. Routing out a grid of circular finger pulls keeps the detailing crisp by eliminating the need for door hardware.

and angles, interior spaces unfold to reveal unexpected views. In many ways, the design of the loft also reflects the dramatic aspects of the homeowner's profession: Michael is a choreographer.

IN THE WINGS

Entering the loft is a little like going on stage. Once inside the front door, you're in a small vestibule. Compared to what's visible beyond, the quarters feel a bit close; the ceiling seems low and the walls press in. To one side, there's a storage room. On the other, panels of wood stained matte black lead to the living room. The impression is akin to waiting in the wings of a theater.

Take a few strides across the cork-tiled floor and the scene changes. Standing in the kitchen, it's apparent that the ceiling in this part of the loft isn't low after all—it's the floor that's higher. Putting this half of the home on a platform is a dramatic way of defining spaces without resorting to walls, which would not only block off views through the loft but also smother the one source of daylight. From this perch overlooking the living room, the vistas become diverse and dynamic—a lively contrast to the "flatlander" perspective of single-level spaces.

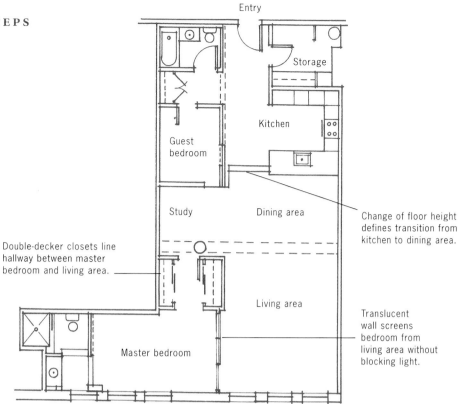

Entry

Storage

Kitchen

Guest bedroom

Study

Dining area

Change of floor height defines transition from kitchen to dining area.

Double-decker closets line hallway between master bedroom and living area.

Living area

Translucent wall screens bedroom from living area without blocking light.

Master bedroom

CENTER STAGE

Step down to the main level, shared by the dining and living areas, and the theatrical atmosphere really comes into focus. Seen from this lower vantage point, the full 11-ft. 3-in. height of the space can be appreciated. The kitchen, with its shimmering backdrop of stainless-steel cabinetry, seems to sit on a proscenium. Over by the windows, another chorus of materials joins the architectural ensemble. Framed in steel, a wall of translucent glass panels lets the living room and the bedroom share light. Bordering it, stretching from floor to ceiling, a band of stacked acrylic rods sparkles in the sun. What gives this collage its punch is its restraint, both in the limited number of ingredients and their selective placement.

BACKSTAGE

The tempo decreases in the compact master suite, which sits on the other side of the glass/acrylic wall. The short hallway that links it to the living area is put to productive use with double-decker closets. Compared to the loft's main space, where the full palette of finishes is evident, this is a restful, almost meditative room. Completely white, its most striking feature is the luminous wall. Frosted glass makes an encore appearance on the far side of the room; a sheet of it is suspended on rollers, which closes off the bath from the sleeping area.

Small as it may be, the master bathroom displays a reprise of all the design elements found throughout the loft. It's got a change of floor height: The toilet and the shower enclosure are a step up from the sink area. Materials are modern but far from sterile—1-in.-square

ABOVE Tall spaces can be emphasized by changes in floor levels. Two steps up from the rest of the loft, the kitchen is kept fundamental. The floor-to-ceiling cabinets afforded by tall spaces are as much irresistible as they are essential for storage-starved urbanites.

green glass smalti cover the walls of the stall and the backsplash, and the basin and vanity doors are brushed stainless steel.

The series of thresholds found in the loft is significant for a couple of reasons. They work as spatial markers, delineating different areas as one goes through the apartment. While they're aesthetically pleasing, they're also functional. Slabs of slate make a durable, waterproof floor at the entry and in the guest bath. In the kitchen, cork tiles underfoot help keep the cook comfortable, as they slightly cushion stand-up tasks; they also absorb noise. Hardwood cherry flooring in the living and dining areas resists the wear of foot traffic.

WHEN IS A WALL NOT A WALL?

In the context of city homes, there are several replies to this architectural riddle.

One: when it's not constructed of conventional materials, like so-suburban drywall. Imaginative materials add a visual accent that's in step with the of-the-moment urban spirit and are a simple way to update a tired interior. Strips of wood veneer woven together, corrugated fiberglass

panels, laminate surfaces, and metal mesh are just a few of the possibilities. Without consulting with an architect or other qualified design professional, these are best employed in non-load-bearing walls. Even when they are used as just "wallpaper," it's a wise idea to check for safety- and fire-code compliance.

Two: when you can see through it. Translucent materials let light

penetrate into spaces that "solid" walls would otherwise render dark. In Michael's loft, 1-in. acrylic rods are stacked horizontally in a frame, like transparent Lincoln Logs. Scrims of sheer fabric are easy to build and to install and make an arty disguise for less-than-perfect walls. Tinted, frosted, patterned, or molded glass can transform the quality of light in a room. If breakage is a concern,

Framed in steel, a wall of translucent glass panels lets the living room and the bedroom share light.

LEFT Wall or window? In some cases, architectural ambiguity does double duty. Acrylic rods and rectangles of fixed translucent glass separate space while diffusing light between the master bedroom and the living area.

look for tempered panes or sheets or investigate acrylic alternatives.

Three: when it moves. Similar to temporary partitions such as portable room dividers, permanent wall installa-tions can be mobile. Especially in loft settings where traditional doors are out of place, pivoting sections of wall can separate one space from another. A series of bypass panels can slide on tracks set into the floor, promoting flexible—not fixed—boundaries. Less problematic to install, panels that are hung from overhead tracks excel at cordoning off smaller areas.

A GLASS ACT

DESIGN CHALLENGE > *to bring light to the potentially dark interior of a row house*

OPPOSITE The clean lines and sharp planes of modern design don't tolerate irregularities well, if at all. Throughout this home, the frames for all the glazing—windows, walls, and doors—are precisely aligned.

RIGHT Part of the urban experience is wondering about the secret worlds behind walls. Few would guess, judging from its solid front facade, that the rear of this house is mostly glass.

Take a random stroll through the residential neighborhoods of any city and you're sure to notice a mix of architectural styles. Without getting academic about it, two broad schools of expression stand out from the hodgepodge of mostly undistinguished dwellings. Some homes, graced with classic ornament and rich in detail, are courtly reminders of the past. Others challenge viewers with their exploration of contemporary creative directions. Of course, there's room for both—the ongoing dialogue between the old and the new is part of what gives a city its dynamism.

ARCHITECTURAL EVOLUTION

This home in Baltimore's Federal Hill district belongs to the second category. Most recently it was a parking garage; a hundred years ago, a trio of 15-ft.-wide town houses occupied the site. Seeking comfortable quarters for their family of five, homeowners Pam and Patrick selected architect Rebecca Swanston to take the structure into the 21st century.

FIRST FLOOR

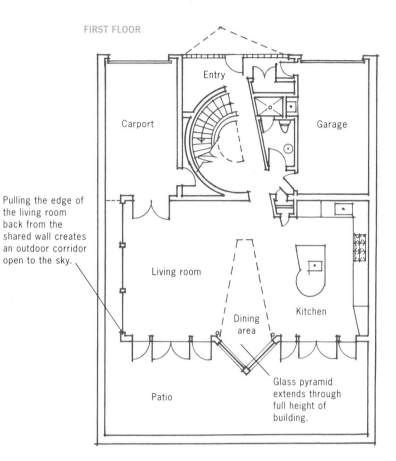

Pulling the edge of the living room back from the shared wall creates an outdoor corridor open to the sky.

Glass pyramid extends through full height of building.

SECOND FLOOR

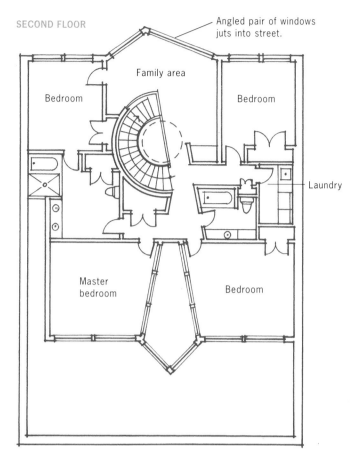

Angled pair of windows juts into street.

Laundry

ABOVE The illusion of space can be exaggerated with a trick as simple as using the same flooring material inside and out.

Metaphorically speaking, it practically zooms there. On the street side of the building, an angled pair of windows juts out from the second story in the sole, subtle hint of what's to come. It's fully revealed only upon walking through the house to the back room, where a pointy wedge of glazing set in an aluminum frame rules over the combined kitchen/dining/living area. Its prowlike outline knifes out of the rear of the building, into the patio. In elevation, it's a cross between a pyramid and a rocket ship, reaching 33 ft. into the air. The glazed element isn't just a flash in the plan; it plays a major role in the new home.

TWO-STORY WINDOW CAPTURES LIGHT FROM ABOVE

Row houses maximize their interior space (and minimize construction costs) by sharing their side walls with their neighbors. The usual consequence of this arrangement is, obviously, a paucity of daylight in the middle of the floor plan. Hemmed in on both sides and, at 45 ft., much wider than the typical town house, Patrick and Pam's home would have been doomed to the same dim fate but for the towering light well, which draws sun into the core of the building.

While the open plan of the ground floor easily accommodated the window structure, the conditions were decidedly different upstairs. There are four bedrooms on the second story, one located in each corner of the building. The interior walls of two of them directly

ABOVE Open plans occasionally suggest a location for specific functions in a space. For instance, the dining table and chairs fit snugly in the alcove formed at the base of the glass pyramid.

face each other across the shaft, raising the question of how to supply the rooms with the privacy they needed without blocking off the sun. The solution: The walls that open to the light well are striated into four horizontal bands of three materials. The bottom layer is wood, which is then topped with panels of frosted glass. These are capped off with two rows of clear glass. The mullions of the interior window walls line up with those of the exterior, creating a seamless appearance.

PULLING IN THE WALL
LOSES SPACE BUT GAINS LIGHT

One of the common walls was the focus of another design decision that had a significant impact on the feel of the ground floor. In the living area, Pam and Patrick could have built out the room to the

ABOVE With no windows in their shared side walls, row houses have a tendency toward dark interiors. Penetrating through the roof and running down to the ground floor, a glass shaft solves that problem in this home.

limit—that is, all the way to the exterior wall. Doing so, they would have gained about 60 sq. ft. of indoor space. The alternative concept (which they ultimately approved) called for pulling the living room back approximately 3 ft. from the shared wall, creating an outdoor corridor that's open to the sky—and thus establishing an ideal opportunity to continue the glass wall around the back to the side of the building. Although this scheme sacrifices some floor area, its benefits are considerable. It brightens the downstairs, improves the balance of natural light, and counters the potentially overwhelming solid mass of the architecture with transparency.

All the design "punch" isn't concentrated at the back of the house. While the glass wall certainly dominates the project, another

LEFT Standard-size features are in danger of being dwarfed by big spaces. To compensate, some dimensions in this kitchen were adjusted: Wall cabinets are hung higher than the norm and the counters are 30 in. deep.

OPPOSITE Well-crafted architectural impressions can deceive in a peculiarly positive way. While this living room physically ends at the window, perceptually it extends to the brick wall beyond.

ABOVE AND RIGHT Contrasting forms keep spaces interesting. The curving, sculptural stair accents this house's otherwise angular environment.

CUT THE NOISE

There are two types of noise in the city: street sounds and those that originate inside a building. Each requires a different solution.

For street noise—most bothersome for ground-level residences, like Pam and Patrick's home— replace loose or worn lengths of window weatherstripping. Reinforce old single-pane windows with a well-sealed storm window, or even better, upgrade to double-glazed units. Don't underestimate the sonic-neutralizing power of a humming fan or air conditioner.

To temper indoor sound, seal off the obvious openings through which noise travels. Start by checking how tightly doors close, and install rubber-gasket sweeps to close any gaps. Consider replacing hollow-core doors with solid ones; they're better sound blockers. Adding a layer of dry-wall to one or both sides of a wall can also be effective.

A caulk gun is a potent weapon in the war against racket. Draw a bead of acoustical caulk around window and door jambs and along baseboards. Take the faceplates off electrical outlets and switches, and squirt the seam where the boxes meet the wall. If you think all this is wasted effort, remember that sound travels

element introduces it in terms of how the space flows. Just inside the front door, a spiral stairway literally throws a curve into the otherwise angular plan, and sets up a diagonal view all the way through the home to the glazed rear facade.

THE CHALLENGE OF
IN-CITY CONSTRUCTION

The building's midblock location created a logistical challenge during construction. The situation could be likened to painting oneself into a corner, except, of course, there was a particularly urban escape plan. The house's new steel framing was all in place, ready to receive the components of the rear window wall. With no side access to the property, a crane was used to hoist sections of the framework over the shell and into the patio, which was used as a staging area for the assembly and installation.

ABOVE Personal priorities can be the deciding factor on how best to utilize outdoor areas. This stamped concrete patio seamlessly continues the living space outdoors and acts as a private playground.

through the air, so damming up even small holes will go a long way toward solving the problem.

Complete the quest for quietude with sound-absorbing upholstered furniture, rugs, and draperies—the softer the surface, the better.

Of course, an effective step in the fight against noise is to make a little noise yourself: In the time-honored metropolitan way, complain to the authorities. Many types of aural irri-

tants, such as commercial air conditioners, construction cacophony, and nightclub blare are limited by local government agencies, and the offenders can be cited and ordered to clean up—or rather, quiet down— their act or face fines.

THINKING INSIDE THE BOX

DESIGN CHALLENGE > *to define spaces and add interest to a high-ceilinged, boxlike loft*

OPPOSITE Starting with a big, empty box, a basic way of ordering horizontal and vertical spaces needed to be established. The solutions are a mezzanine hung across the rear of the loft and a wall of polished plaster slicing through its 19-ft. height.

With telecommunications facilities—the so-called "telco hotels"—snapping up much of what remains of the vacant-warehouse stock, those in search of the loft life are finding fewer and fewer vintage buildings on the market. In an attempt to satisfy the demand for flexible, high-ceilinged settings, real-estate developers are increasingly invoking the "build it and they will come" credo, with the resulting new construction generally falling into two categories of housing.

The less visionary of these efforts proffers prefab, stereotyped style in the form of gratuitously exposed ductwork and unimaginative open floor plans. Another class of construction is the shell building, subdivided into unfinished units that are primed for the occupants to customize. Although not endowed with an age-burnished atmosphere, these environments are structurally sound, meet code standards, and boast modern amenities (such as fire sprinklers, central air, and energy-efficient windows) that would be shockingly expensive to retrofit in an older building. Basically blank slates with a certificate of occupancy, they provide a solid framework for more adventurous expressions.

MEZZANINE

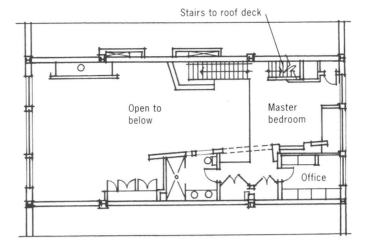

Stairs to roof deck

Open to
below

Master
bedroom

Office

Positioning the stairway against the
side wall conserves floor space.

FIRST FLOOR

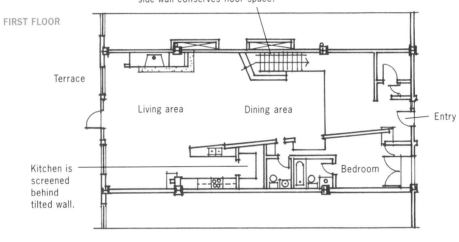

Terrace

Living area

Dining area

Entry

Kitchen is
screened
behind
tilted wall.

Bedroom

BELOW Flamboyant or
Zenlike, campy or elegant,
the tone of a home's design
is set by its entrance. Here,
a high-low-high rhythm to the
volumes leading into the
main living area is a powerful prelude to the striking
space of the loft.

BREAKING UP THE BOX

Bob's Boston home is located in one of these shell buildings. It's a
cross between the row house—with its windowless, shared side
walls—and a commercial space, with a footprint of 63 ft. by 27 ft. and
ceilings of 19 ft. While its dimensions are indisputably industrial
scale, the converted-loading-dock look has been passed over in favor
of a far more cultivated aesthetic, created by Ruhl Walker Architects.

Stepping in from the central access corridor, an intense series
of contrasting spatial experiences awaits. A shaft of sun hits the floor
just inside the front door, at the bottom of a light well that stretches
up to the ceiling. In the next few feet, a mezzanine suddenly drops
down over the dining area, cutting the height of the space in half.
Just as abruptly, the ceiling opens up again, continuing over to the far
wall of windows. What's the upshot of this sequence of varied enclosures? It energizes what would otherwise be a big but boring void
and also introduces a second, smaller scale into the space, which is
easier to inhabit than the intimidating, full 19-ft. height.

TILTING THE WALL ENLIVENS THE DESIGN

The vertical axis also has a major design element that's injected into the space: a towering, tilting wall of polished plaster. Listing and angling into the floor area, it's both a sculptural object and a spatial organizer, partitioning off bedrooms, baths, an office, and kitchen on the ground and upper levels. If the wall had been standard-issue plumb, it would simply repeat the boxlike circumstances the architects were trying to correct and avoid. The wall has several niches and slots cut into it; most of these openings are filled with translucent glass, hinting at the spaces beyond. Bolstering its mystique, the wall seems to hover over the dark brown oak floor, adding to the delicate feeling of ambiguity generated by the architecture.

RIGHT Walls don't have to be mere surfaces for displaying art—they can be art themselves. Hand-troweled and finished with a coat of beeswax to add luster, this plaster wall, with its exacting composition of glazed openings, becomes an artistic object in its own right.

ABOVE An open plan doesn't mean everything has to be on view. So as not to compete with the purity of the main space, the kitchen— with its relative busyness of cabinetry and appliances— sits out of sight, selectively screened by the tilted wall.

A WALL OF WOOD

If you follow the contours of the plaster wall to where it ends in the living area, another monolithic plane comes into view. A wall of door-size maple panels backs up the kitchen, the wood bringing a note of warmth to the room. The grid lines are not simply decorative; they're actually the edges of storage closets that can be reached via a utility ladder. The straight seams also serve as a reference point from which to appreciate the curve and tilt of the plaster wall.

Using rich, color-saturated natural materials, like black granite and red oak finished in a brown satin stain, sets up a contrast with the white walls. They work almost as a background, reinforcing the impression that the walls have been slipped into the empty space of the loft and are independent of its confines.

Using rich, color-saturated natural materials, like black granite and red oak finished in a brown satin stain, sets up a contrast with the white walls.

PERSONALIZING THE PLAN

At the developer's invitation, homeowners were given a chance to make some changes—at their own expense—in the design of the basic building, as long as they could be implemented in the planning phase or early stages of construction. In the case of Bob's loft, the decision was made to flop the plumbing stack to the opposite wall, a move that allowed the floor plan to be laid out to better capture the skyline views.

Installing skylights was another alteration to the unit's original plan. With a double bank of northeast-facing windows climbing nearly the full height of the 19-ft. space, the sun angles fairly deep into the open, ground-floor areas. But to brighten and enhance the quality of daylight in rooms located on the mezzanine, additional sources of light were needed. Ruhl Walker strategically placed four skylights in the roof. One, as mentioned before, is centered above the entry; it also benefits the bedroom. Others illuminate the dressing area and the master bath, where a sandblasted glass wall in the shower is subtly backlit by a skylight over the kitchen.

ABOVE In the master bath's shower, a large panel of translucent glass is bisected by a band of clear glass, allowing a peek at the living space below.

ABOVE Getting the right amount of natural light into a space takes some doing. On the back side of the mezzanine, two of the bedroom's "walls" are open railings, letting the area benefit from sun on three fronts: a skylight, interior clerestories, and the windows on the far side of the loft.

TIPPING THE SCALE

With so many apartments and lofts carved out of existing spaces, it's hard to find a place that isn't in need of some help when it comes to issues of comfortable scale. Here are some pointers on how to deal with a less than perfectly proportioned space.

Too shallow/short/narrow? Begin by stripping away every extraneous detail that stops the eye as you scan the space: trim, paneling, moldings, light fixtures, even doors (if they're absolutely necessary, try the pocket variety). By definition, unobtrusive, built-in furnishings are a savvy choice over freestanding pieces because they keep the perimeter of the room clean; bookcases are a particularly wise use of limited space.

Using a single, continuous material for flooring and countertops perpetuates a seamless look. Strategically placed mirrors and reflective surfaces are one of the oldest tricks in the book—and for good reason: They work, especially when utilized in conjunction with windows, where they can help blur the distinction between indoors and out. Lastly, painting a room in pale colors will bounce light through it, emphasizing the elusive (and illusive) sense of airiness.

LEFT In this view from the mezzanine, it's clear how floating ceiling and wall planes at slight and differing angles gives shape to the space. Doing this makes the interior much more compelling than if all the boundaries were left in their original parallel state.

Too long/tall/wide? An excess of even awkward space is a "problem" many would like to be burdened with, but it does have its drawbacks, as Bob's loft illustrates. Because the solutions usually involve serious construction rather than a cosmetic fix, it's more costly to correct this condition than it is the too-small scenario. One of the ways to cushion spatial shock is to build an elevated platform (in addition to improving dimensional definition, there's storage space to be gained). Depending on the size of the surrounding room, this could range from a false floor or crawl space of 18 in. to something considerably more substantial.

Thoughtfully situated, nonstructural partition walls can segment overly expansive areas into a logical floor plan. Dropping in a mezzanine or gallery level creates additional living space while tempering extreme verticality. As far as colors are concerned, darker palettes will lower ceilings and tighten spaces, but they should be used judiciously—otherwise, they will absorb all the light in a room, resulting in a residential black hole.

part 3

apartments

URBANE RENEWAL

DESIGN CHALLENGE > *to divide a town house into apartments with a garden view*

OPPOSITE Timeless proportions are appropriate in settings modern, traditional, or in-between. The living room of this apartment—orthogonal, divided into thirds—comfortably transcends its 1832 origins.

New Orleans has a reputation for elusiveness: What you see is not necessarily what you get in this chimerical city. Certain hallmarks of the local architecture—enclosed gardens, shuttered doors and windows, and hidden courtyards—contribute to its enigmatic air, which is a compelling blend of friendly flirtation, a touch of mystery, and a recurring element of surprise.

The renovation of this 1832 town house bears this out: The residences behind its red-brick facade are delightfully unexpected in their design. The architecture firm of Errol Barron/Michael Toups took charge of rescuing the building from its previous incarnation as transient lodgings and turning it into apartments, with each apartment having the opportunity to enjoy the rear courtyard.

In order to do so, and to maintain an adequate amount of living area (the units are each about 1,800 sq. ft.), it was necessary to exercise some creativity with the layouts of the individual homes. Because there is a service wing extending off the back of the main building, there was some room for flexibility in the floor plans. The apartments were designed as duplexes, but instead of stacking the living spaces directly over one another in typical fashion, the levels are offset, with each unit divided between the front and back of the building.

Another challenge that presented itself was how to make the project architecturally interesting without resorting to either a blood-

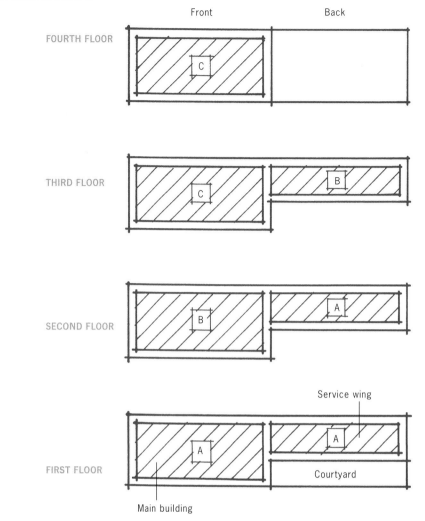

FOURTH FLOOR

Front | Back

C

THIRD FLOOR

C | B

SECOND FLOOR

B | A

Service wing

FIRST FLOOR

A | A

Main building | Courtyard

ABOVE The typical side-by-side arrangement of town houses isn't ordinarily conducive to admitting daylight. Thanks to the offset position of the service wing in the back of this house, the sun evenly enters all three floors of the building. Balconies, running the length of the annex, work like outdoor corridors, linking spaces laterally.

less reproduction of a period interior or a scheme that completely ignored the building's historic nature. The course finally taken acknowledged this building's 19th-century character while simultaneously taking a progressive tack. It was decided to focus on specific geometric elements of the old house and pare them down to purer, more contemporary forms.

JOHN'S APARTMENT: RESHAPING THE INTERIOR

A few blocks southwest of the Vieux Carré, the building sits in the heart of the resurgent Warehouse District, which has gotten a firm toehold as the city's latest hot spot. Galleries, cafes and restaurants, artist studios, and shops have gradually sprung up throughout the blocks of old cotton mills and storage buildings. In keeping with the new fabric of the neighborhood, a fine-crafts gallery occupies the street-front space of the three-story Georgian structure. Half of John's apartment sits above the gallery on the second floor (the rest is situated one story up in the service wing, overlooking the garden). The living room runs across the width of the house and is brightened by

ABOVE AND BELOW Offering relief from the same-old-square-room scenario, the circular dining room (below) has a less static atmosphere than the standard space. Spicing it up even more is another interior window (above), a direct reflection of those on the front facade.

ABOVE Framed artworks aren't the only way to ornament a wall. This interior window in the living room (one of two) balances the room's composition and anchors a sitting area. It opens onto the bath, hence the translucent glass.

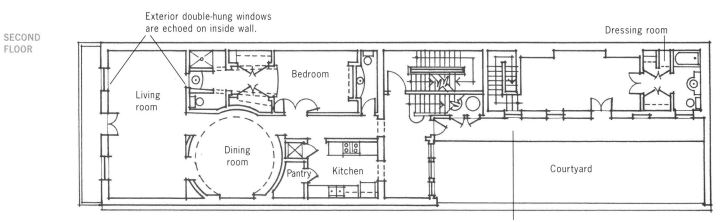

Exterior double-hung windows
are echoed on inside wall.

Dressing room

Living
room

Bedroom

Dining
room

Pantry   Kitchen

Courtyard

Balcony overlooks courtyard.

ABOVE Buildings (and not only those in New Orleans) are adept at keeping secrets. Swing open the mirror in the bathroom and a window is revealed, its frosted panes providing light as well as privacy from the living room it looks onto.

RIGHT Built-in niches not only enliven a room architecturally by defining specific shapes and spaces, but they can also conserve room in confined areas. Note how the nightstands are floated in the openings on either side of the bed; the niches swallow what would have been furnishings protruding into the room.

two large double-hung windows that flank a French door. In an intriguing detail, these windows are echoed on the opposite, inside walls of the room. Repeating them in this way sets up a resonance with the original building and adds a fresh feeling of lightness to the space.

One of the windows is filled with panes of translucent glass; in true New Orleans fashion, this arouses a curiosity about what lies beyond. In order to keep the bedroom relatively dark—a request of the homeowner—it had to be set back from the front windows as much as possible. Therefore, the bathroom was placed between the window and the living room. The configuration of the room increases that dimension: The bath and adjacent dressing area/closet sections are stretched out so that they are long and tapered, in an elongated wedge instead of a box. For privacy's sake, the interior window was occluded.

Across the hall is the dining room, with its own window looking out onto the living area. It too breaks away from routine, right-angled chambers. It's more or less a rotunda, with a slight flattening on one side and a pronounced soffit around the perimeter. Like the bathroom corridor, the circular shape conceals several minor cosmetic faults in the existing structure. While the house was structurally

sound when the renovation started, like most elderly buildings, it was punctuated with the idiosyncrasies that occur over time: doorways a little crooked, floors a bit sloped, and the like. Enveloping these small flaws in new interior construction compensates for the discrepancies between reality and ideal conditions—another example of the influence illusion plays in the Crescent City.

ABOVE As they settle and sag, the crooked quirks of older houses are to be anticipated in any renovation. Here, inserting a wholly different geometry—the circular form of the dining room—absorbs the slack between the irregularities of the building's outer shell and the revamped interior configuration.

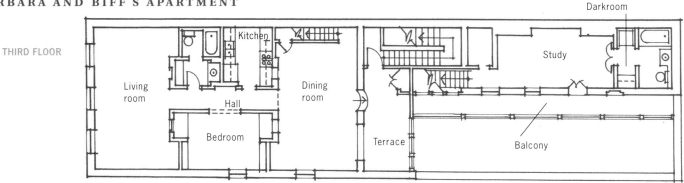

THIRD FLOOR

Darkroom

Kitchen

Living room

Dining room

Study

Hall

Bedroom

Terrace

Balcony

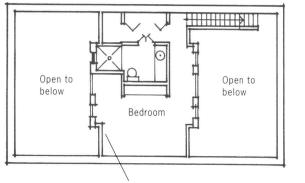

FOURTH FLOOR

Open to below

Open to below

Bedroom

Half-walls allow light into windowless upper floor.

ABOVE In this dual-purpose building—the oldest structure in Faubourg St. Mary—access to the residences is made through the door off to the side of the gallery on the ground floor.

ABOVE In remodeling projects, large-scale changes yield equally big results. Eliminating the attic in this 170-year-old town house opened up the vertical space for a freestanding two-level structure.

BARBARA AND BIFF'S APARTMENT: A HOUSE WITHIN A HOME

With the back half of the top story occupied by the upper level of John's duplex, the third floor faced a shortage of square footage unlike anywhere else in the building. In solving the problem, Barron/Toups designed a kind of whimsical homage to the town house itself, one that takes the architects' focus on the underlying figures of the building to its fullest expression. A scaled-down version of the entire structure was erected that nearly fills the front section of the main house. But it's not a carbon-copy replica; rendering the mini-building in plain drywall stylizes it and emphasizes its basic sculptural forms, without the distractions of texture or color. (It has subsequently been altered, with some of the details and lines now smoothed into a slightly less articulated, more abstract composition.)

It was decided to focus on specific geometric elements of the old house and pare them down to purer, more contemporary forms.

LEFT AND BELOW Manipulating the quality of space—raising or lowering ceilings, compressing or widening corridors—invigorates the spatial experience of a home. Walking through the new mini-building sets up an appreciation for the open double-height volumes that surround it. Functionally, it's a compact, self-contained guest quarters, with a loft bedroom (left) and laundry facilities (below right) contained in the stylized, scaled-down representation of the structure.

COMBINING APARTMENTS

As demand for urban homes continues to hold steady, it can be a challenge—both logistically and fiscally—to find larger quarters that maintain a consistent quality-of-life condition. An increasingly popular alternative is for residents to annex space in adjacent floors or apartments.

The first step is a delicate one: inquiring if the neighbors are interested in selling. In the interest of

diplomacy, it is best to have a third party, such as a real-estate agent who is familiar with the building, broach the subject in writing. The purchase price in such arrangements is often higher than it would be on the open market, but the net value of the combined units is often greater.

Going forward, an accurate set of architectural documents needs to be compiled. Even if you are

able to put your hands on a set of original blueprints, there's a fair chance—particularly with an older structure—that they may not reflect the current state of the building and its mechanical systems. It's a sound investment (indeed, one that's a prerequisite for remodeling) to have a new set of measured drawings made.

What can and can't be done in an apartment merger varies by

A corridor cuts through the middle of the house-within-a-house, allowing passage between the living room and the dining room. It contains a full bath and kitchen on its "ground floor," with a bedroom and bath with shower upstairs. Half-height walls wrap the edges of the upper level, permitting light and air to flow freely through the space, as well as facilitating face-to-face contact between people in the loft and those down below.

While a sleeping loft is a common corrective action in studio apartments when additional living area is needed, it's a rather novel approach to take in a town house—and in this case, one that required some structural alterations. To make room for the two-level construction, the original attic was removed and the roof restructured. While swapping storage for extra breathing room is often a difficult decision to make in city quarters that are pressed for both types of space, when the payoff is as innovative and aesthetic as it is here, you can't lose.

ABOVE AND OPPOSITE Synchronizing a remodeling with the building's strong points is key to a fully successful design. In this case, the exterior galleries that run the length of the service wing on both upper floors allow openings in the interior to take full advantage of the natural light.

location, with both individual building management and city departments weighing in. Vertical expansions, for instance, may not span more than two floors, but when the growth is contained to a single floor, more than two units may be combined—as long as the total number of rooms in the enlarged apartment does not exceed the total before the renovation. Typically, one kitchen must be closed and its plumbing connections capped. Another common restriction prohibits what's called "wet-over-dry" construction: putting a bathroom over a closet in a neighbor's home. Some cities require that a new certificate of occupancy be obtained when combining units.

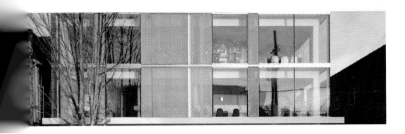

RESIDENTIAL MEETS RETAIL

DESIGN CHALLENGE > *working on a small site with restrictive zoning regulations, to design an elegant mixed-use building on a budget*

OPPOSITE It isn't unusual for building codes to play a causal role in the layout of a floor plan. Sometimes this poses a problem, sometimes not. Mandated fire walls more or less dictated that the areas of this home that were to be enclosed by window walls—the living/dining spaces—would have to be positioned on the southern and eastern exposures.

As complex and costly a process as it may be, constructing a city home from the ground up certainly has its advantages. It's possible to benefit greatly from the latest technology, often resulting in a building that's more efficient in its design, execution, and short- and long-term maintenance. And of course, as a custom-made work of architecture, you're in the position to realize most, if not all, of the features on your wish list.

Naturally, there's a flip side to new construction as well. Perhaps the principal drawback has to do with site selection. In the competitive world of urban real estate, it's not always practicable to obtain a parcel that's ideal in terms of price, location, and size. To some degree, compromise is always part of the picture. Having a clear understanding of one's fixed priorities, as well as what points are negotiable, can help cut down on the frustration level. Home-owners set on building from scratch are well served to be open to alternatives that may crop up during the search for the perfect lot.

OFFICES AND AN APARTMENT

This project in Portland, Oregon, brings together lessons from both sides of the issue. As a mixed-use structure—one in which commercial and residential spaces co-exist under one roof—the building makes a real commitment to urban living. Its three floors of retail

and office square footage topped by a duplex apartment are an investment in both a home and the community.

Homeowners Ann and Robert have a living situation that requires flexibility in the present as well as in years to come. Prominent in the design business and supporters of the arts, they do a fair amount of entertaining at home. On a personal note, they will find themselves empty nesters in the not-too-distant future. So while the house needs to work well for large social gatherings, ultimately the couple will be its primary occupants. The challenge: Create an interior that's spacious and flowing but that still retains a sense of comfort and scale that's suitable for two people.

STRUCTURING THE DESIGN

Allied Works Architecture recognized at the outset that the lot's size and attendant zoning restrictions would exert a strong influence on many aspects of the building's design. The firm evaluated various structural systems, from heavy timber to concrete, before settling on a steel-frame solution, deeming it the optimal choice with regard to cost and ease of assembly on the cramped infill site.

Several applications for variances to height, setback, and other standards were made to enhance the functionality as well as the aesthetics of the plan. For instance, winning an appeal on the 45-ft. height limit—the ruling stated that the limitation need only apply to the bulk of the building, which in turn facilitated the construction of a fifth-floor penthouse with generous setbacks—had a ripple effect on the floor-to-floor heights of all levels in the structure. They range from 10 ft. to 12 ft. tall, with the tallest floors the residential ones.

CODE REQUIREMENTS HELP SHAPE THE PLAN

Building and safety codes also contributed to shaping the floor plan, beginning with how the home is entered. Instead of a front or street-side door, one walks behind the shop on the ground level to an elevator; access to the residence is made on the fourth floor, then an internal stairway leads up to the top story. The decision about where to situate the apartment's public and private spaces was largely made by the code requirement for fire walls on the north and west sides of

ABOVE Walking into a home is like meeting a person: First impressions count, a reality that's underscored if the residence is frequently used for hosting business associates, as is this abode. The view from the elevator entrance establishes the tone of this apartment: modern but not cold, elegant but not stuffy.

the building; floor-to-ceiling glazing wraps the living and dining areas to the south and east, while fire-resistant masonry protects the bedroom, bath, and study. In order to gain natural light and views, select portions of these walls—for example, off the bedroom and bath on the fourth floor and the master bath on the top floor—were pulled inward about 5 ft. and glassed in.

It's in the open areas of the living room and kitchen/dining space that the fine line between large and small scale is most publicly tread. To provide a gracious proportion within the height restrictions, several of the interior walls stop short of the ceiling. Light and

ABOVE When planning an original work of architecture, an honest assessment of the homeowners' lifestyle is particularly important in a function-oriented room like the kitchen; otherwise, efficiency is sacrificed. In this apartment, the owners regularly hold catered events, so an open-galley arrangement with plenty of counter space makes a lot of sense.

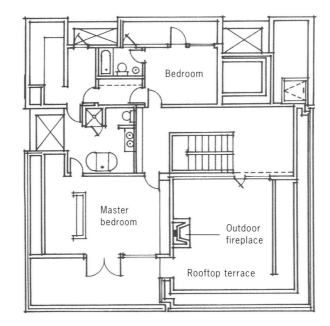

FIFTH FLOOR

Bedroom

Master
bedroom

Outdoor
fireplace

Rooftop terrace

FOURTH FLOOR

Entry (via
elevator)

Interior stairs

Interior walls
stop short of
the ceiling to
allow light
and air flow
around them.

Kitchen   Dining area   Living room

Balcony

Floor-to-ceiling
windows wrap
the living and
dining areas.

ABOVE Used with confidence and intelligence, materials can give definition to different zones throughout a home. Here, a wood-sheathed corridor divides the apartment's public spaces from the family's private quarters. An eccentric "welcoming committee" is framed in the often-awkward void under the stairway.

air flow around them, moderating their effect on the rooms. It's less choppy, more continuous, and extends the reach of the window walls. Still, it's their carefully calculated lengths that work to moor the space and channel the views throughout. The balance struck between vertical and horizontal and between transparent and solid makes the space an easy fit for intimate gatherings as well as for lively crowds.

BREAKING THE MOLD

Taking into account the clients' penchant for modernism, the architects at Allied Works looked for ways to expand the themes of openness, imaginative use of materials, and connection to the outdoors. Such a treatment boldly breaks the local stylistic mold for this type of building; similar mixed-use projects in the neighborhood tend

toward mere imitations of historical looks. Here, the building's presence is accentuated by countering its mass with elements emphasizing transparency. An envelope of glass and metal mesh is slipped over the structural steel grid, blurring the edges of the building and thus making it seem larger—and lighter—than it actually is.

On the main level of the apartment, the links to the great outdoors are primarily visual, limited to what can be seen through the window walls. There is a narrow balcony right off the living room, but it's pretty much "standing room only," useful mostly as a favorite vantage point for guests. A stairway leads up to a more expansive (and private) outdoor space. Claiming nearly a quarter of the area of the fifth floor, a rooftop terrace complete with fireplace provides an open-air retreat off the master bedroom.

SHADOWS AND ILLUSIONS
IN A MANHATTAN APARTMENT

DESIGN CHALLENGE > *to create a stimulating but soothing environment inspired by living in a high-rise*

RIGHT AND OPPOSITE Walls don't have to meet in a predictable fashion nor must they be made of pedestrian material. An intersection of unexpected ingredients and dimensions, such as these opaque surfaces and volumes giving way to transparent and translucent planes, achieves the same function—a simple division of space—but in a thought-provoking way.

It's widely touted as one of the ultimate urban compliments: "Philadelphia (or San Francisco, or some other deserving destination) is a great walking city." Where low-rise structures account for much of the city's interesting architecture, the cityscape is best seen and appreciated from a pedestrian point of view. But things change quickly in the big city. Ever since skyscrapers, once the exclusive domain of big businesses, became vertical residential neighborhoods, we've never looked back (or down). With the help of technology and Dramamine, we've adapted to this unnatural perspective like the axiomatic duck to water.

PLAYING WITH PERCEPTIONS ENLIVENS THE DESIGN

This home, which is located in a Manhattan apartment tower, is the site of a project that examines the perceptual consequences of living high in the sky. Dean/Wolf Architects seized on a quality intrinsic to the apartment—its very "apartness"—and made it the basis for many of the design ideas that are explored in the remodeling. The city inspires but does not impose itself on the space; a

The city inspires but does not impose itself on the space; a permanent yet shifting distance is maintained between the two.

BELOW Dining areas demand a sense of enclosure; meals are a time to connect with friends and family rather than stare out the window. While the end walls of this apartment are all glass, there are solid walls at its core, which give an element of intimacy to an otherwise expansive, airy space.

permanent yet shifting distance is maintained between the two. Up on the 30th floor, this abode is isolated in the air, with all physical connections to the city severed. Its relationship to the immediate environment, then, is on a purely visual level, limited (at first thought) to what can be seen through the window walls to the east and west. The architects sought fresh ways to work those vistas into the composition of the home and in turn channel their energy throughout its rooms.

The footprint of the apartment is roughly rectangular in shape; you enter at the midpoint of one of the long sides and are greeted by a sleek, built-in aquarium. The square tank sits at eye

level, flush with the wall that encloses the galley kitchen. It's lined up with the kitchen window, so during the day the fish appear to be swimming in space. That impression (and other illusory variations on it) recurs throughout the home as part of the ongoing emphasis on three kinds of images that enliven the design: reflections, projections, and shadows.

ABOVE A modern rendition of the mirrored wall trick: By reflecting images of the skyline, the glazed partitions pull the vitality of the city into the apartment visually, but unlike the infinite reflections of a looking glass, they contain it within a flat surface.

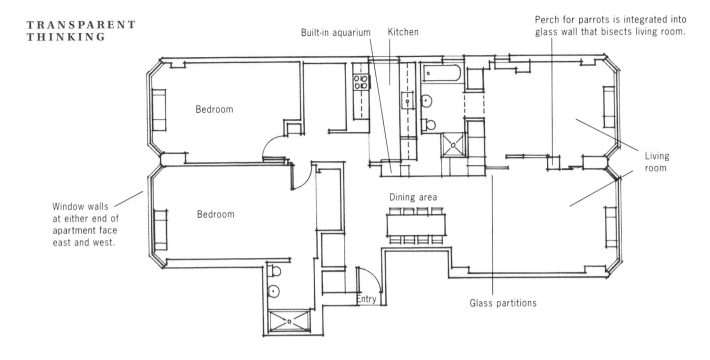

Built-in aquarium   Kitchen

Perch for parrots is integrated into
glass wall that bisects living room.

Bedroom

Living
room

Window walls
at either end of
apartment face
east and west.

Bedroom

Dining area

Entry

Glass partitions

ABOVE AND OPPOSITE In apartments with walls
that are substantially glass, the appeal of exterior views can literally fade away with nightfall.
Here, with the advent of darkness, the attraction shifts inside, with the illuminated fish tank
(above) and video projections (opposite) appearing miragelike in the living and dining spaces.

A PIVOTING GLASS WALL IS A CAPTIVE SCREEN

A wall of glass bisects the living room, but it's not fixed in place;
there's a pivot hinge at each end, with the plates coming together
in an L-shaped notch. Panels of sandblasted and clear glazing are
combined, so there's a slight variation in texture and depth. Largely
transparent, the wall doesn't promote privacy; it acts primarily as a
canvas or screen for the different types of images, each of which has
its own optical characteristics. First, it captures the crisp reflections
of the skyline. Oriented to the west, the living room looks out onto a
dozen or so marquee properties, among them the Empire State
Building and the gilded pyramidal roof of the New York Life Insur-
ance Co. While the scene is reminiscent of an oversize museum dio-
rama, even from behind glass it's charged with visual drama and
intensity. Moving and repositioning the panels to catch the reflections throughout the day and night lets the homeowner manipulate
the view and the vision.

   A video player that's concealed near the top of the south wall
projects films onto the translucent portions of the glass panels, in a
surreal, miragelike effect. The same areas also pick up shadows cast
by objects that are caught in the sunlight. Lacking the sharpness of
detail that is visible in the reflections and the projections, the soft
gray forms add a slightly mysterious, abstract element to the room.
Among the items regularly silhouetted are the homeowner's two
parrots, who take pride of place on a custom-fabricated stainless-
steel armature that hangs from the ceiling; complete with seed pan,
it's a very cosmopolitan perch, indeed..

ABOVE AND RIGHT Locating rooms strategically means taking stock of personal preferences as well as aesthetic ones. Placing this master suite on the eastern exposure allows the owner to wake to the sunrise and the soothing sight of the river, rather than confront the jumble of skyscrapers to the west.

ARCHITECTURE FOR ANIMALS

Dean/Wolf describes the relationship between nature and this apartment's parrot roost and fish tank as idiosyncratic; certainly, there is an unnatural aspect to fish and birds residing 30 floors up in the air. Still, on another level the provisions couldn't be more pragmatic: They directly respond to these animals' needs. As people seek comfort and stimulation in their urban homes, animals living in the city merit the same consideration; after all, they spend more time cooped up in the house than do their owners. Just as in plotting a design for humans, take into account the abilities, likes, and dislikes of your pets, and plan their environment accordingly.

For example, as curious, independent, agile creatures, cats are best served and entertained by structures that appeal to these qualities. What could be better than a catwalk to engage the feline both physically and mentally? An inclined ramp leading up to a raceway that meanders around the perimeter of a room—

Largely transparent, the wall doesn't promote privacy; it acts primarily as a canvas or screen for the different types of images, each of which has its own optical characteristics.

BELOW With forethought, the needs of pets can be accommodated by the design, avoiding unsightly compromise later. A perch for the birds has been integrated into the design of the glass wall, casting the animals and the architecture into complementary roles.

The resulting range of images—distorted, realistic, ghostly, symbolic—give the apartment an identity that's both distinct from and dependent upon the surrounding city. The experience of being in the living areas, in particular, is certainly dreamlike, akin to being in the clouds: The apartment hovers in the sky; the fish float in their tank and the birds in the air. A frame from a motion picture glows ethereally on the wall, which, as it's made of glass, does some levitating of its own.

A contrast is found on the eastern side of the high-rise, with its relatively placid views of the river, lit in the morning by the sunrise. As a place for rest, the bedroom is more sheltered from the visual forces that play in the public areas of the apartment, and the choice of finish materials bears that out. Wood and stone veneers face the walls: tactile, nonreflective surfaces that ground the space rather than activate it.

or rooms—just a foot or so from the ceiling provides a private realm that's also filled with ever-changing vantage points. A semi-enclosed observation pedestal located near secured, sunny windows is a kitty-size retreat that's portable. Carpeted surfaces help increase traction and soften sleeping platforms.

Dogs, having to make relief trips outdoors on a daily basis, are a different story. Their regular walks—supplemented by excursions to neighborhood dog runs where they are free to gambol, socialize, and generally exalt in their dogness—satisfy much of their exercise needs. Owners who have the means and

space to indulge their faithful companions further can take inspiration from New York's famed Biscuits and Bath Doggy Village, where the facilities include an AstroTurf running track (complete with a mechanical bunny to chase), an obstacle course with hoops and hurdles, and a lap pool.

ELEVATING THE DESIGN
OF A CHICAGO HIGH-RISE

DESIGN CHALLENGE > *to update an underdeveloped high-rise unit hampered by structural restrictions*

OPPOSITE Cookie-cutter apartments may be the most economical to construct, but they usually leave much to be desired in terms of aesthetic appeal. Here, carefully plotted manipulations of walls, doorways, and ceiling planes turned a nondescript condo into a home with genuine presence.

In the late 1980s, a decreasing demand for residential real estate caused a lot of developers to hedge their bets when putting the finishing touches on their downtown projects. Concerned that the condominium market would stay soft, many sought to contain their losses by cutting back on the design and construction of their buildings—not in ways that would undermine safety but in ways that would sap any aesthetic interest. It's the ripple effect of this attitude that was responsible for the unrealized potential of Steve's two-bedroom, two-bath apartment; it's also what set the course for its remodeling.

The corner views this 30th-floor aerie commands are anything but humdrum. The vistas are classic Chicago: The John Hancock Tower rises to the north; from the living room a glittering stretch of Michigan Avenue can be observed; and on the eastern exposure, one can view Lake Michigan and a panorama of residential towers.

To elevate the apartment's design so that it would be on a par with its inspiring surroundings, architects Brininstool + Lynch had to clear a number of hurdles that are native to tall, modern buildings. Among the offenders here are odd and awkward angles, low ceilings, and structural columns and walls that intrude on the space at the most inopportune points—for instance, the pentagonal hunk that pushes into the window wall of the living room. Because these condi-

tions were immutable, the floor plan remained largely unchanged as the design team zeroed in on its task. The team's approach centered on transfusing the sterile atmosphere of the condo with one of sophistication, something that would generate a sense of anticipation as people look and move through its rooms.

SMALL CHANGES YIELD BIG RESULTS

Instead of abruptly opening onto one another, the spaces were designed to gradually unfold and reveal themselves. Since major structural changes were out of the question, sliding and swinging doors—think of them as small, moving walls—were used to gently reshape the space and give the rooms some flexibility that wouldn't be possible with fixed partitions. The architects also chose materials that would soften the transitions between areas and cultivate a strong feeling of serenity. One of the principal tools they employed was translucent glass; as the main component of the new doors, it spreads a visual calm while it diffuses light throughout the apartment. The only tweaking of functions concerned the second bedroom, which was to be used mainly as a home office and library yet still be available for service as part of a guest suite.

Overall, the remodeling goes a long way toward debunking the notion that interior architecture is all about grand gestures and floor plans that make a Big Statement. Subtle changes in proportion and

The architects chose materials that would soften the transitions between areas and cultivate a strong feeling of serenity.

BELOW Buildings turn corners in different ways: some good, some plain goofy—done for outward appearances and engineering necessity rather than interior appreciation. A chunky structural column in the living room is sheathed in anegre wood, a major part of the design scheme.

BELOW The key to getting the maximum amount of flow from a floor plan is to create wide, embracing openings between rooms. In this residence, the relationship between the bedroom and living room was transformed by removing the old wall between them and installing a less rigid boundary of translucent glass doors.

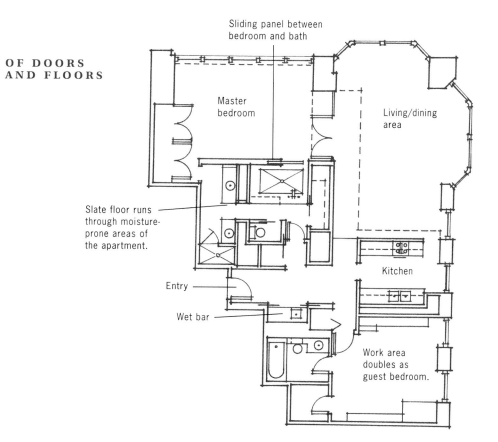

Sliding panel between
bedroom and bath

Master
bedroom

Living/dining
area

Slate floor runs
through moisture-
prone areas of
the apartment.

Kitchen

Entry

Wet bar

Work area
doubles as
guest bedroom.

feel were achieved by minor but precise alterations of each of the
wall and ceiling planes, doorways to rooms were repositioned by
mere inches to align and free up sight lines, and walls and soffits
were extended or shaved down by similar increments to strike an
aesthetic balance. While this restraint was to a great extent mandated
by the existing construction, it also supported one of the prime
objectives of the job: to enhance the dramatic views.

BEHIND CLOSED DOORS

A wet bar (an urbane invention if there ever was one) located in the
entry corridor provides an example of how the strategy was applied
throughout the apartment. Originally open to the hallway, its over-
haul began with building out the wall a bit in order to accommodate
a set of pocket doors made of translucent glass and steel as well as to
hide some indirect lighting fixtures. When the doors are closed and
the lights are on, an impression of a deeper space—perhaps there's
another room beyond?—is created. Like the rest of the home, the
bar's proportions were refined and its materials changed. The cabinetry was reconfigured and constructed out of anegre, a creamy-tan
hardwood with a low-gloss luster. Used in almost every room of the
residence—for the bathroom vanities, the headboard of the bed, and
the wall paneling—the wood makes an important visual contribution
to the design.

On a larger scale, the master bedroom benefits from a similar
treatment. A 9-ft. portal now links it to the living room and sports
frosted-glass doors of the same design as those of the wet bar. The

ABOVE Introducing new elements—particularly where the floor area is limited or confined—may require some trade-offs. Here, a small hallway was eliminated to make room for the expansive tub in the master bath. Thanks to a sliding-glass panel, it enjoys a view through a corner of the bedroom and out to the living-room windows.

effect of the luminous panels is more easily imagined if one considers the banal alternative: a stock 3/0 door plunked into a blank stretch of drywall.

The master bathroom was the only room that was expanded by any significant amount. It was enlarged by claiming a former hallway as the spot for a rather special new tub fabricated of stainless steel. The tub sits on a raised platform in the bathroom, which is separated from the master bedroom by a panel that can slide closed for privacy or can remain open when a peek at the scene on Lake Shore Drive is wanted.

The facelift was completed with a round of customized camouflage, which focused on overcoming the throwaway detailing that characterized the old condominium. In particular, the heating, ventilation, and air-conditioning units presented a special challenge; their clumsy, wall-mounted grates begged to be disguised. Grilles were crafted out of steel to help seamlessly merge function and form. The metamorphosis finished, the home can now hold its own against its distinguished neighbors.

SMALL APPLIANCES

With the trophy-stove crowd the exception, much has been made of urbanites' tendency to treat their kitchens as vestigial spaces. When the forces of time (not enough of it) encounter the realities of space (not enough of it, either), something's got to give. For many, take-out and delivery services have effectively rendered cooking at home to the history books.

Nonetheless, there's a full range of scaled-down appliances that can give a closet-size kitchen like Steve's all the functions of a full-size room. Most of them are available by special order through dealers.

Refrigerators. The ConServ 375 stands 78 in. tall and can squeak into a space that's less than 24 in. wide. Because it also measures 24 in. deep, it fits flush

LEFT It's not always necessary to gut every room of the home to revitalize it. This kitchen received just a simple sprucing up. The existing cabinets were reused, light fixtures were updated, and a new slate floor laid down, which runs throughout all the moisture-prone areas of the apartment—bathrooms, entry corridor, and kitchen.

with standard cabinetry. For the ultimate in inconspicuous appliances, Sub-Zero's refrigerator-in-a-drawer can be custom-finished to blend in with your cabinets.

Dishwashers. The compact theme continues with Fisher & Paykel's DishDrawer, a full-cycle machine contained in a pull-out drawer. A standard-installation, slim-line appliance from Miele is a mere 17½ in.

wide, yet holds eight place settings. The Spacemaker model from General Electric fits directly under the sink, putting what's usually remnant space to work. Countertop washers appeal with their minimal size (one manufactured by Equator is about 20 in. by 20 in.) and portability, but they must be hooked up to a faucet.

Laundry. The stacking washer/dryer unit is a classic for apartment

dwellers. General Electric makes one with a bifold lid that allows unencumbered access to the tub—very handy when you're stuffing a week's worth of clothes into it. It also features a built-in light, so you won't miss your target with the Spray 'n Wash.

A HOUSE FOR ENTERTAINING

DESIGN CHALLENGE > *to strike a balance between closed-off rooms and an open floor plan*

Ann and Howard had outgrown their previous residence, a town house in the vicinity of Philadelphia's Rittenhouse Square. Over the course of their two-year-long search for a new, larger city abode, the couple had been able to refine just exactly what they did and did not want in their new home. Ann was standing firm on her desire for some sunny outdoor space, something she could turn into a kitchen garden. Howard was focused on finding a place that was in move-in condition, dead-set against getting involved with any property that needed remodeling—even one that begged only for a change of wallpaper.

So it came as quite a surprise to them both that the totally gutted, top two floors of a commercial building that was being converted into apartments should capture their collective fancy. While roof rights could give Ann her garden, it was clear that they would have to undertake a complete rebuilding of the space to turn it into a

OPPOSITE In this home, strong rectilinear lines show off the intense color and grain of the woods used in the cabinetry. Book-matched panels take this to a higher level of artistry.

RIGHT The public spaces in this duplex were located on the upper floor because of its superior natural light sources.

SOCIALLY STRUCTURED

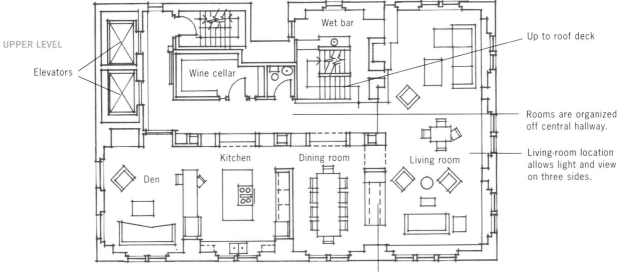

UPPER LEVEL

Elevators

Wine cellar

Wet bar

Up to roof deck

Rooms are organized off central hallway.

Den

Kitchen

Dining room

Living room

Living-room location allows light and view on three sides.

Pass-through wall divides dining room and living room.

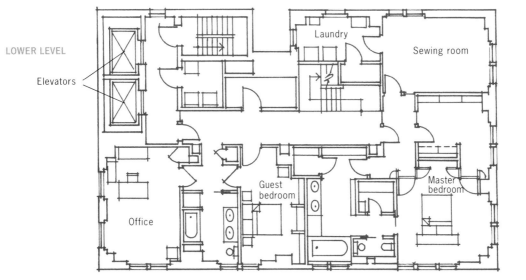

LOWER LEVEL

Elevators

Laundry

Sewing room

Office

Guest bedroom

Master bedroom

Rooms on lower level are conventional in plan.

LEFT As seen from the living room, the central corridor's role as a spatial organizer is clear. Befitting its high volume of foot traffic, its floor is finished in durable slate.

ABOVE Varying the degree of visual tension—from jarring effects to subtle illusions—keeps a space from becoming stagnant. In this duplex, measured compositions of solids and voids, patterned and plain surfaces, colors and whites play off one another to create a stimulating (but not overly active) atmosphere.

home; even utility connections would have to be made. But as a tour of some other apartments in the 16-story building confirmed, it offered the opportunity to create and control their environment instead of continuing to hunt for a home that would likely be less than a perfect fit. The potential for achieving that—and more, as pointed out by architect Christopher Beardsley—ultimately overrode any preconceived objections.

ROOMS ARE OPEN YET SUBTLY SCREENED

Because the couple entertains on a regular basis, it was important that the duplex be designed to comfortably accommodate a fair number of people, rather than be a sterile showcase for objects. Family quarters, conventional in plan, are situated on the lower level of the residence; the upper floor was designated as the social space because of its high ceilings and good natural light.

The den, kitchen, dining room, and living room are laid out in an L-shaped plan along two outer walls, with the living room occupying the entire base of the L. This location gives the living room the benefit of windows on three sides. It's also farthest away from the elevator, making the walk through the floor to reach it a process of anticipation. And it's convenient to the stair leading to the roof deck, another spot for gathering.

The rooms are organized off a central corridor, but in order to keep the spaces fluid and friendly for guests to navigate, these

LEFT Layers of space challenge the observer's eye and are more interesting than simple voids or a warren of rooms. Clearly defined spaces can be achieved without resorting to light-blocking walls by employing a three-dimensional grid of columns and counters, along with a varied palette of materials.

Together, the screen and columns set up a series of vistas that changes as one moves throughout the floor.

ABOVE There is a middle ground between the wide-open quality of a loft and the enclosures of a traditional apartment. A freestanding screen wall, with solid base and open shelves above, softly structures the space without boxing it off.

rooms are not succinctly closed off from one another nor are they left undifferentiated by being blended into an open plan. A balance is achieved by using a strategically designed and located screen wall, which divides the living room from the dining room. It is a partition that is solid from the floor up to about waist level, then opens into an elegant composition of pass-through—and thus see-through— shelves. It promotes the visual connection between spaces while gently defining the physical separation.

Complementing the screen are the columns that make up one side of the corridor: Rectangular in shape, substantial in size, and buttressed with short lengths of counters, they're more of a miniwall than supporting posts. Together, the screen and columns set up a series of vistas that changes as one moves throughout the floor.

ABOVE Treated consistently, even the tiniest details can unite a space. Small circles become a hallmark of this otherwise thoroughly orthogonal home: Seen in the wooden inlays on the walls, the column girder, and the handrail as well as the bolts on the base of the balustrade, they regularly dot the interior.

RIGHT AND BELOW Varying the type and amount of finishes throughout an interior can underscore a room's place in the hierarchy of the home. For instance, while the public areas upstairs are done mostly in bright, light woods, the family's private spaces downstairs are more subdued in tone. In the master bath (below), cool slate dominates. Marine blue walls give the bedroom a restful feeling (right).

MATERIAL MATTERS

From the dining room, a view of the stairway is framed. This vantage point well illustrates the interplay of materials found in the apartment. Clear maple covers selected vertical surfaces, brightening the areas where it appears. Sections of the ceiling and cabinetry are finished in panels of anegre, a hardwood whose rich, reddish grain is emphasized by intricate, symmetrical installations. Underfoot, tiles

ROOF DECKS

When creating an urban arboreal aerie, you'll be contending with some environmental conditions that are more extreme than they are at ground level, as well as some aesthetic issues unique to rooftops.

Container gardens are good for bringing spots of color—or even masses of color—to the roofscape. Fiberglass planters withstand the freeze/thaw rigors

of northern climes and stand up to heat and sun equally well. Grouped together, the pots also comprise a handy screen against vent pipes. Wheeled plant trolleys can make repositioning the containers much easier, not just to capture the sun but to allow access to the vent stacks. Less portable but more effective for camouflaging vertical surfaces, vines trained to climb up sturdy

trellises can help hide unadorned chimneys and walls.

The plants have to be secured against whipping winds, as does everything else on a high-rise terrace. Built-in features, like the perimeter seating at Ann and Howard's home, aren't a concern, but patio sets should be made out of cast iron or other heavy, durable material; forget about flimsy resin tables and chairs.

of moss-green slate add texture and durability to the stair treads and to the floor of the high-traffic hallway.

Color, always a handle-with-care element in interior architecture, plays a deliberately limited part in this design. Following the tenets of feng shui, Beardsley assigned rooms specific hues that are meant to underscore their function. For instance, a yellow wall channels energy to the area surrounding the wet bar, while a backdrop of crimson in the dining room is used to encourage good conversation as well as hearty appetites.

A quick climb up the stairs leads to the roof garden. The cedar deck was installed by laying it down on a dozen pallets, which were then set on the surface of the roof. The weather-resistant wood was also the material of choice for built-in benches, which act as bookends to a row of eight planter boxes containing herbs and ornamental grasses. An intrusive wall that encloses the rooftop mechanical systems is softened by incorporating it into a shade-making pergola.

Avoid using umbrellas for shade, because even models with weighted bases can become airborne. A more stable alternative is a retractable, cantilevered awning that is affixed to the building. Pergolas, arbors, or similar garden structures, sturdily constructed and anchored in place, are other possibilities.

"Permanent botanicals" (the professionals' term for artificial plants) are gaining some ground in city gardens due to their ultralow maintenance. No vigilant fertilizing or watering is necessary; all the plastic posies need is an occasional hosing down. Originally used by hotels and restaurants, they're increasingly popular with homeowners; one New York City couple retains a gardener (perhaps better described as a technician?) to perform monthly upkeep on $20,000 worth of phony foliage, including adding and removing blossoms when the seasons change.

town houses

A TALE OF TWO STORIES

DESIGN CHALLENGE > *to keep living and work spaces separate in a house built within a modest budget on a tight infill lot*

In any city, there are usually several threads of architectural styles running through the urban fabric. In Toronto, with its historic ties to Great Britain, a variety of English-influenced expressions flourished in the 19th and early 20th centuries, among them Georgian, Victorian, and Edwardian buildings, stately and formal in character. Things changed as the 20th century progressed, though, when the International style arrived on the scene; from then on, the earlier styles gradually waned to the point where they are now mostly limited to institutional edifices.

This iconoclastic house in the neighborhood of Danforth Village flies in the face of traditional design. Shim-Sutcliffe Architects took various elements of the Victorian cottage and, in the boundary-pushing spirit of the city, interpreted them with a decidedly urban edge.

RIGHT AND OPPOSITE The floor plan works to intensify and internalize the urban condition, rather than follow the typical, single-family house mold. Instead of a front door off an elevated porch, the entrance to this home is at the center of the plan, at ground level.

LEFT New construction adds to a city's layers of history, sometimes in surprising ways, such as with this town house. There's symbolism behind the two types of siding. The marine plywood panels sheathing the upper half of the building are a nod to the commercial loft, while the clapboard cladding below recalls the traditional Toronto cottage.

LIVING AND WORK SPACES ARE SEPARATE BUT TOGETHER

When commissioning the project, Robert, the homeowner, came to the table with an exceptionally clear and detailed concept of how the house needed to work. An architect, researcher, and archivist, he wanted living and office spaces under one roof but separate from one another. As the functions differ, so do the environments—and while it's a strong contrast, it's also a comfortable one, owing to the consistency of the architecture. There's a unity of materials, detailing, and overall aesthetics throughout the house, which transcends the dimensional differences between the two floors.

BELOW Ambience isn't just a function of decor; scale and color play important roles, too. In Robert's kitchen, as in all the rooms on the ground floor, low ceilings and bold colors create a cozy atmosphere, which is reinforced by the austere cabinetry and lighting treatment.

The design scheme uses the fundamental elements of light, color, and volume to give the interior a dynamic sense of contrast.

A real-world budget forced the construction process to be direct and the design to the point. But that's not to say it was a corner-cutting procedure by any means. On the contrary, the constraints helped the client, contractor, and architects to work together as a team and address issues with discipline and creativity. The structure would be economical, with wood framing and concrete-block basement walls on a concrete slab. This back-to-basics focus allowed for several custom-fabricated splurges: a skylight over the stair landing, mahogany windows, and a copper exterior light fixture.

The site for the house was a vacant infill lot, which measured just 25 ft. wide. Side-yard setbacks to the north and south were fixed at 3 ft.; by petitioning for a variance of 1½ ft. along the north side, room was gained for a garden on the southern flank.

LOW CEILINGS AND WARM COLORS
MAKE FOR COZY LIVING QUARTERS

The spatial division of the home is simple: Each floor plays a different role. Turning the conventional organization of the cottage upside down, the ground level is the domestic realm and the work room is upstairs. While the arrangement reflects a degree of symbolism, there's also a pragmatic underpinning to it. At the outset, Robert had identified in broad strokes the types of spaces he wanted: cozy living quarters and an airy, light-filled office. Shim-Sutcliffe came back with a scheme that uses the fundamental elements of light, color, and volume to give the interior a dynamic sense of contrast.

Downstairs, walls and ceilings are painted in rich hues that emphasize the intimacy of the spaces. A snug 7 ft. 6 in. in height, the bedroom, bath, and eat-in kitchen are detailed in a modernist vein that's more modest than it is machinelike. In the kitchen, the natural-wood cabinetry is pared down to its essence. A band of open boxes is hung along the wall behind the sink. The lighting treatments are equally ascetic, with bare bulbs in pivoting fixtures set flush with the ceiling or, where they're centered over the dining table, recessed into it. While the forms may be minimal, the use of wood and saturated colors gives the room an inviting warmth.

ABOVE Stairways are transitional zones, often possessing a quality distinct from the spaces they connect. Climbing to the second level of this town house, you're immersed in light from skylights above and spotlights at the treads—a signal that a dramatic change of scene is imminent.

SECOND FLOOR

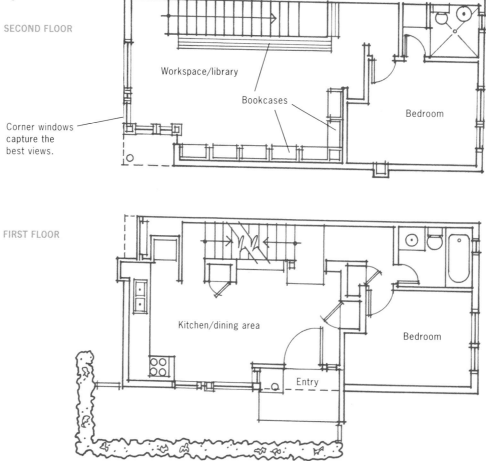

Workspace/library

Bookcases

Bedroom

Corner windows
capture the
best views.

FIRST FLOOR

Kitchen/dining area

Bedroom

Entry

A HIGH CEILING AND A WALL OF WINDOWS
CREATE AN AIRY, LIGHT-FILLED WORKSPACE

Upstairs in the office, it's a different picture altogether. The ceiling now rises to 12 ft. A cool white has replaced the warm color palette of the first floor. The rudimentary cabinets of the kitchen have evolved into an imposing wall of bookcases, which house Robert's library of 2,000 books; 3,000 vertical files; and 65,000 index cards—and, to a bibliophile's delight, there's still shelf space to spare. But the most outstanding feature of the airy, loftlike space is its abundant natural light, the complete antithesis to the dim and gloomy interior that's common with a cottage. In fact, it was the desire (and ability) to control the daylight that led Robert to the decision to build a new residence from scratch, rather than renovate an older house.

The windows that bring the sun inside are strategically placed to capture the best views and are sized to admit the maximum amount of light. The southwest corner of the second floor has been notched away, then glassed in with a mix of fixed glazing and casement windows that open onto a stand of trees. Skylights over the stair and a large window wall at the west end of the floor guarantee that an even amount of sunlight reaches all parts of the room.

BELOW As the functions of the home change between floors, so too do the scale, light, and color scheme. The second story—open, bright, and white—reverses the conditions of the ground level.

ABOVE Every site has its unique conditions that affect the design of the home. Because this house sits on a narrow infill lot, windows—custom mahogany constructions—are concentrated on the ends rather than on the sides of the building. This frames views of the treetops and skyline rather than the blank walls of the neighboring houses.

ABOVE In the city, nature and the automobile are perpetually at odds with one another, but here's a happy exception. By using a special perforated, reinforced concrete block set flush to the ground and seeded with grass, a parking place becomes a parklike space.

Turning the conventional organization of the cottage upside down, the ground level is the domestic realm and the work room is upstairs.

ON THE OUTSIDE

The dual purposes of the 1,100-sq.-ft. town house are also expressed on the outside of the building. Familiar 1x4 wood-plank siding, so often used on the city's cottages, covers the residential half of the home. The second floor is wrapped with full sheets of exterior-grade plywood, a hard-working material that's distinctly industrial.

Finally, while many Toronto residences have garages (indeed, the city requires them to be included in new construction projects), Robert rejected that personal convenience in favor of a design that's more considerate of the public streetscape, as well as environmentally sound. In the front "yard" of the property, concrete blocks with a checkerboard-patterned filigree are filled with turf, providing a grassy camouflage to the parking area. This tactic—the result of a successful appeal to the building department—works especially well for this site, which permits no on-street parking.

SUCCESSFUL STORAGE

The first commandment of creating successful storage: Thou shalt take copious and accurate measurements. Even a straightforward system like Robert's library is predicated on precision: Its 13-in. fixed shelves are tailored for oversize art books. Knowing the dimensions of the objects to be stored—whether it's clothing, cooking paraphernalia, or office equipment—as well as those of the proposed storage area is a solid start to designing an efficient scheme. It's particularly critical in remodeling projects, where tolerances and clearances can be difficult to fit, thanks to existing conditions that are often maddeningly irregular. No matter how careful you try to be, eyeballing or guesstimating will quickly condemn you to overflowing closets and shelves.

Commandment number two: Know thy stuff. Analyze how frequently the objects to be stored are used and organize them accordingly. Things that are in use daily (the coffee mugs, say) should be within easy reach, at eye or waist level. Items that are occasionally needed (mixing bowls, to continue the kitchen analogy) can be stowed just outside that zone, accessible when bending down or reaching overhead. For rarely used objects, like the Thanksgiving soup tureen,

placing them in out-of-the-way locations, perhaps reachable only by ladder, gives priority to items that are in routine use.

Lastly, allow room for your material goods to grow. While at first thought it might seem excessive, a rule of thumb is to anticipate an expansion of 50 percent beyond your immediate needs when planning for storage.

If you ultimately end up losing the battle of the belongings, you may want to resort to a fallback that is especially popular with city dwellers. Off-site storage facilities range from a 4-ft. by 5-ft. by 5-ft. bare-bones locker to climate-controlled rooms suitable for valuable furnishings and soup tureens alike. These can be rented by the month or for longer terms, with rates that naturally vary by facility and location.

BUILT FROM THE TOP DOWN

DESIGN CHALLENGE > *to satisfy a growing family's need for more living space with a one-of-a-kind design*

OPPOSITE An intrinsic problem with open plans is finding a way to design a graceful entry; without a foyer or vestibule, there is scant opportunity to develop a transitional space from outdoors to inside. To mute the most overt aspects of the kitchen, many of its appliances were built into the stair structure, where they're out of view of arriving visitors.

The popular image of Los Angeles as a centerless sprawl of single-family houses, bounded by the ocean and bisected by freeways, is often scoffed at by residents of "real" cities, who are convinced the only meaningful measure of a town can be taken in granite towers, not palm tree–lined streets. But L.A.'s laid-back landscape belies the fact that getting a building built in southern California is no stroll on the beach.

Forces of nature as well as manmade circumstances combine to make it an exceptionally complicated process. Building safety codes, seismic standards, energy regulations, and environmental-impact commissions make L.A. arguably the toughest city in the country in which to build. Lots are small, height restrictions ever-changing, and many communities have their own design review boards attempting to arbitrate style. The architectural upshot doesn't fit the textbook definition of a metropolis, recasting it as a low-rise, high-density locale instead of a concentrated collection of vertical buildings.

PHASE ONE: ADDING A SECOND FLOOR

On a number of fronts, Jonathan and Deborah's home also defies expectations. Construction took place in two distinct stages and in an atypical sequence. Normally, one builds from the ground up; this home was created from the top down. In the first, strictly pragmatic phase, an upper story was added to the 1930s' Spanish-style building;

BELOW Together, modern building technology and aesthetics can give form to exceptional visions; two examples of that partnership are at work in this home. Laminated wood beams more than 40 ft. long span the length of the second-floor study without needing to rely on post supports, which would intrude on the open area. The exposed quality of the walls and ceiling was achieved by installing rigid insulation on the outside of the building's plywood shear diaphragm.

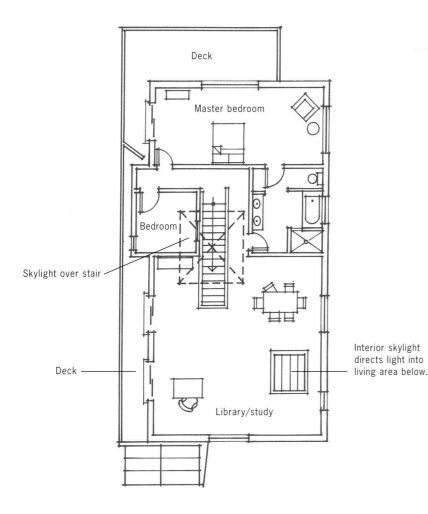

Deck

Master bedroom

Bedroom

Skylight over stair

Deck

Library/study

Interior skylight directs light into living area below.

An upper story was added to the 1930s' Spanish-style building; some time afterward, the ground floor was redone.

BELOW Using elemental materials such as wood or stone is a sure way to bring a sense of the natural to a stridently manmade world. The choice of plywood as a finish produces two divergent effects: Its raw quality evokes an atmosphere of spontaneity in the home, while its precise dimensioning and placement contribute a feeling of serenity to the space.

some time afterward, in a purely aesthetic move, the ground floor was redone.

Another surprise is the singular character of the design itself. To satisfy the growing family's need for more living space, architect John Clagett designed a commodious second floor, containing a library/ study, a master suite, and a nursery. On paper the volumes may sound intimidating—14-ft. ceilings, a 28-ft. by 28-ft. study, a 14-ft. by 28-ft. master bedroom—but when experienced in person, it's an uplifting, one-of-a-kind environment. On one level, the large scale of the space is a challenge for people accustomed to standard, 9-ft. ceiling heights. But at the same time, the room is restful and comfortable, owing to the simple, direct proportions and the repeating patterns of the studs, joists, and panels. The rhythm of the studs, for instance, was slowed by using deeper 2x6s instead of 2x4s and spacing them at longer, 24-in. intervals rather than the customary 16 in.

The space is warmed by bountiful natural light. A 10-ft.-sq. skylight is centered over the stair, and windows are placed high on the walls, letting sun travel across the width of the interior. The bottoms of the windows are aligned with the top of the plywood course (which stands 8 ft. tall), both grounding them and scaling down the space. The extensive use of wood—mostly birch veneer plywood and sheets of construction-grade ply—also has a calming effect on

RIGHT Increasing light levels while preserving privacy is a common urban equation that begs for an ingenious balance. With another building barely 6 ft. away, oversize sandblasted glass doors screen the view and let plenty of light into the kitchen area.

ABOVE Existing conditions always impose a certain number of restrictions on a project; resolved skillfully, they can end up enhancing a home. Because the first-floor space—remodeled after the second-floor addition—could never equal the height of the upper story, the architect decided to emphasize its horizontal lines. One way this was done was by opening up a view through the house, from the front out to the backyard.

the atmosphere of the home, the figure of its grain and modulating colors lending it a harmony and intimacy.

A pair of irregularly shaped pavilions animate the otherwise neutral space of the upper level. Containing the master bath and a child's bedroom, they sit off the stairwell on opposite ends of the floor, mediating the volume of the bigger space with their angular roofs. The bath building stands 9½ ft. high; the roof of the nursery reaches the taller ceiling but in doing so slopes sharply back toward the outside wall. Operable windows and openings in the pavilions' ceilings further the impression that they're self-contained structures, the larger room having been built around them.

PHASE TWO: SUBTRACTING FROM THE FIRST FLOOR

Smitten with the casual, spacious quality of the upstairs, the couple called on Clagett a few years later to transform the ground floor, too. With four bedrooms, three baths, as well as kitchen, dining, and living rooms crowded into a dense, cellular collection of discrete spaces, it was the spatial antithesis of the second story. The transformation required revisiting—and ultimately revealing—the structure of the earlier addition. The second floor was in large part supported by columns that had been slipped into cavities in the downstairs walls. As these walls were now destined to come down to free up the

FIRST-FLOOR REMODEL

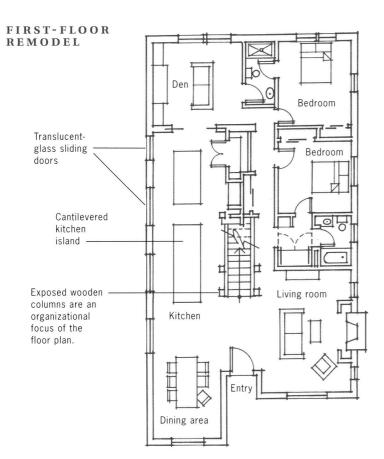

Den

Bedroom

Translucent-glass sliding doors

Bedroom

Cantilevered kitchen island

Exposed wooden columns are an organizational focus of the floor plan.

Kitchen

Living room

Entry

Dining area

ABOVE While a bathroom should have a sense of privacy, that doesn't mean it must be closed in and claustrophobic. The expansive second floor of this home allowed the bath's ceiling to be dropped down considerably; several openings were then cut into it. The result tends to relax the room, blurring the boundaries between it and the larger, "outer" space without compromising its seclusion.

ABOVE A change in scale, materials, and color reinforces a room's identity. Where most of the second floor is big, woodsy, and warm, the master bath is a more intimate space, tiled in a cooler palette.

space, the wooden columns were exposed. They became the points around which the floor plan was reorganized.

On the ground level, the proposed open plan presented two particular problems that called for inventive resolutions. The first was just inside the front door. Eliminating the entry vestibule to maximize the openness of space meant that visitors would step smack into an area that was sandwiched between the kitchen and living room. To keep the kitchen from being too confrontational—after all, an array of major appliances is hardly a welcoming sight—many of its mechanical accoutrements were packaged under the deep, long stair. The refrigerator, an air-conditioning unit, two large microwave ovens, a full pantry, a broom closet, and numerous drawers are hidden away there, out of sight of arriving guests but readily accessible to the cook.

Achieving a comparable quality of light on the first floor as upstairs was another challenge. Despite the fact that there is no view and little privacy on this level (a neighboring residence stands a little more than 6 ft. from Deborah and Jonathan's kitchen wall), a series of oversize translucent-glass sliding doors was installed in the kitchen. The deliberate placement and height of the 8-ft.-tall openings on the west side of the building trumped the potentially sun-blocking structure next door, filling the space with brightness.

SKYLIGHTS

Second only to square footage, natural light is the city dweller's most valued commodity. Because of their full, flat exposure to the sun, skylights are far superior to windows when delivering the most light to the greatest possible area. Their benefits go beyond brightening a space; by visually removing a section of the roof, the perceived volume of a room is immeasurably increased. The sky's the limit.

Made of glass or acrylic, skylights are available in a wide range of standard sizes and can be installed on roofs that are nearly flat up to a pitch of 85 degrees. To make them more energy efficient in warm, sunny parts of the country, they can be ordered with low-e glass and fitted with indoor shading accessories.

Heat and moisture buildup can be controlled by specifying operable, rather than fixed, models. Sizable lights, like the 10-ft. by 10-ft. one in Deborah and Jonathan's home, can be motorized for convenience and practicality. Operable skylights have other pluses: They admit fresh air into a space and promote good vertical ventilation, allowing hot air to rise out through the top of the structure.

Windows are placed high on the walls, letting sun travel across the width of the interior.

One other feature worthy of mention is the glass stairway. Enclosing a stairway in glass certainly tests the limits—especially in a region prone to earthquakes. Motivating the pursuit of this improbable detail was the knowledge that had the stair been built of an opaque material, it would have cut off the passage of light and obstructed the open space in the heart of the home. Using engineering principles more often found in the design of skyscrapers, trapezoidal sheets of tempered glass were assembled into a transparent shaft. While compliant with the most demanding of building codes, it stands as a pure expression of creative vision.

BELOW Roof-mounted skylights are the conventional way to bring overhead light into a home; an interior skylight is an innovative extension of that concept. Meticulously engineered for strength and safety, a section of the upper-story floor sandwiches a panel of wire glass between two sheets of tempered glass and directs light from the second-story library down into the first-floor living area.

Insect screens can be fitted on the inside opening of a skylight to shut out unwanted winged guests.

Special configurations, such as domes, barrel vaults, pyramids, and ridge structures, can be custom manufactured—for a handsome price, of course. The impact of these forms is two-fold: Not only can they be appreciated when seen from below but from outside the building as well, making a small, crystalline contribution to the skyline.

INDUSTRIAL MERGER

DESIGN CHALLENGE > *to turn a pair of commercial buildings into a live/work space while maintaining the character of the original structures*

Sage and John are retired, but they remain actively involved with causes and consulting projects that reflect their interests. Sage, a dancer for most of her life, now heads up a leading foundation in that field. John, previously a publishing executive, is engaged in a variety of pursuits. While their myriad professional and social activities exempt them from the rocking-chair set, they were tired of having to maintain separate offices, traveling to them daily from their home. The couple was ready to consolidate this far-ranging pattern, and started looking for a place that could accommodate their soon-to-be-streamlined lifestyle.

In addition to needing ample space for the combining of their offices and home, they wanted an environment that reinforced their affinity for the simple, tactile technologies of the 19th century. It was

RIGHT AND OPPOSITE
Visual texture—variety in scale, style, details, and materials—gives a particular energy to the urban scene. Inside this house, that mix is demonstrated by leaving structural elements exposed: steel posts and beams, open ceiling joists, and pipe railings.

—

ABOVE Joined together, two 19th-century structures—a former electrical contractor's shop and a stable—comprise this Minneapolis residence. The faded painted sign reflects the homeowners' wish to respect the commercial character of the buildings as much as possible.

partly this sensibility that helped them recognize the potential in a run-down pair of attached brick buildings in a then-forgotten area of Minneapolis. A former electrical contractor's shop stood perpendicular to the street; a onetime horse barn was connected to its far end. The ground floors were filled with junk, the roofs (where they were still intact) leaked, wood elements were rotting, and sections of the masonry were crumbling. But despite all this, the melancholy appeal of the property—and its secluded yet central location—still shone through.

PASSING THE "FLASH TEST"

The architectural firm Meyer, Scherer & Rockcastle worked with Sage and John on this unusual project. The stable—the more derelict wing of the building—was gutted and essentially rebuilt. The home's ambience, it was agreed, would remain true to the building's blue-collar

RIGHT Living and working under one roof requires a well-ordered floor plan to function optimally. The ground floor is where the couple's offices and studio are located; the living spaces are upstairs.

ABOVE Sometimes the choice of materials can work on an immediate level (how it completes a room) and on a broader one (how it ties in with the philosophy behind the building). For example, a perforated metal screen separates the kitchen from the living area, and the material adds an industrial edge to the home.

ABOVE By design, the building incorporates architectural "accidents" that were made by previous tenants. For instance, rather than even out the floor levels where the buildings were originally joined, the master bedroom sits a few steps up from the second story.

ABOVE Although it's more common to connect two buildings side to side, attaching them at a right angle poses interesting design possibilities. Here, the entry and stairway mark the point where the stable and workshop were mitered together. Frosted glass keeps the office shielded from view.

origins. In fact, the influence of an invisible third party was felt throughout the planning process. The question "What would Mr. Flash have done?" became a yardstick for design decisions. It's a reference to the electrical shop's namesake, who, judging from the state of things, apparently favored the expedient over the artful when it came to maintaining the property.

The result is an unabashedly plebeian palette of materials—corrugated sheet metal, concrete block, and rubber flooring—applied to a basic plan. By taking such a low-key approach, Sage and John were able to achieve the unassuming impression that was so important to them. In the interest of authenticity, worn surfaces and materials were repaired rather than replaced wherever it was feasible. The wood floors were preserved and patched; spalling brick was plugged with mortar. When new materials were introduced—as in the kitchen, where panels of perforated metal screen separate the kitchen from the stairwell and the living room beyond—they were chosen for their compatibility with the industrial atmosphere.

Even the significant additions and alterations were kept tightly in character. For instance, on the second floor where the two buildings were originally joined many years ago, the new doorways leading to the bedrooms are deliberately out of proportion; they're a shade wider and slightly shorter than would normally be expected. This is in keeping with the unaligned floor levels that occurred when

In the interest of authenticity, worn surfaces and materials were repaired rather than replaced wherever it was feasible.

the pair of structures were originally cobbled together, a condition that required the architects to raise a small area of the roof to gain sufficient headroom.

Access to the building was moved off the street, from the end of the electrical shop to near the crook where the two sections of the structure meet. Sheltered by a plain, metal shed roof, the entry sets a casual mood that's more "employee entrance" than formal front door. It's also a secure, convenient point at which to enter the home. Workspaces are kept to the ground floor, so deliveries and visitors aren't traipsing through the family's private quarters. Access to the upstairs living areas is made via a new stairway just inside the door,

BELOW In a holdover from the existing buildings, the floor plan was kept open. Now, instead of promoting commercial productivity, it lets people and activities flow easily between the adjoining living, eating, and cooking spaces.

FIRST FLOOR

Glass panels screen office from entry vestibule.

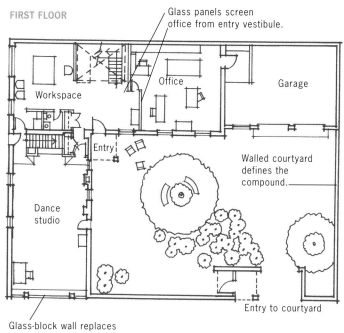

Workspace

Office

Garage

Entry

Dance studio

Walled courtyard defines the compound.

Entry to courtyard

Glass-block wall replaces original entrance to electrical shop.

SECOND FLOOR

Perforated screen panels separate kitchen from stairwell and living area, and let in sunlight.

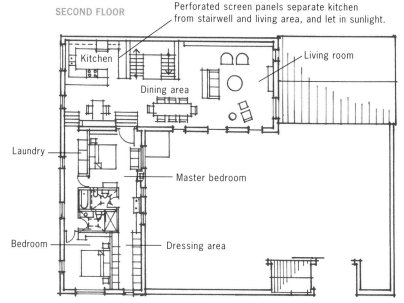

Kitchen

Living room

Dining area

Laundry

Master bedroom

Bedroom

Dressing area

ABOVE Not all home workspaces are centered around a desk and a computer. The glass-block wall in Sage's dance studio is where the original entrance to the electrical shop was situated. When it was closed off, a mix of clear and translucent block passed the "Mr. Flash test" for architectural integrity; it provides light without sacrificing privacy.

sparing guests the sight of a busy office space. On the second level, the plan is filtered yet again, where it's separated into a public and a private wing.

WINDOWS OLD AND NEW LET THE LIGHT IN

The different ways natural light was introduced throughout the building are no exception to the ad hoc aesthetic. While the back wall of the stable was without usable openings, most of the existing windows have been preserved, with some of them enlarged. The couple's workspaces received close attention. In the dance studio, where good illumination and visual privacy needed simultaneous solutions, a large field of mismatched glass block was laid on the end wall. John's office is separated from the entry vestibule by a steel-framed wall of glass panels, which borrow light from the adjacent stairwell. The portions of the home where light is especially important to safety are given special consideration. Over the central stair, a sawtooth skylight jags up to capture the daylight, while boxy twin funnels resembling grain hoppers rise from the other wing, directing the sun into the baths.

On the outside, the compound hardly aspired to be the belle of the block, but its L-shaped plan did beg for completion. The lot was large enough to accommodate a garage and a yard. In another act of studied slapdash, a utilitarian metal-roofed shed was appended to the

LEFT Where modern materials were introduced into the design, they had a factory feel to them, such as the rubber disk–tread flooring in the office.

former stable. A cinder-block wall was erected around the boundaries of the property, creating a secure, secluded courtyard. In true Flash fashion, the courtyard is surfaced in asphalt instead of grass.

FROM BACKWATER TO BOOM

Since they moved in, Sage and John have embraced the diverse quality of downtown and have seen the once-ragtag blocks around their home gradually develop. Even as mixed-use neighborhoods—those that have a vibrant blend of commercial, industrial, and residential buildings—become more popular with municipal planners and city dwellers, Sage and John's neighborhood boasts a tenant that's especially arresting: The Metrodome rises just 400 yd. away from the couple's home.

The sports complex is a contemporary anchor to the eclectic nature of the area, which includes a paint factory, a hotel-turned-office building, and a warehouse that's now the locus for several non-profit literary organizations. Sage and John's pioneering home is still the ultimate exemplar of this funky mix.

LEFT After delineating work from social spaces, a second degree of separation occurs within the social realm. The private parts of the house—bedrooms, baths, dressing area, and laundry— are sequestered in one wing of the L-shaped plan, away from the public areas.

GRAFFITI

Although it hasn't been an issue at Sage and John's residence (sports fans in certain other urban centers are less benign than their Twin Cities' counterparts), graffiti can be a problem in neighborhoods through which large crowds pass.

There are some steps homeowners can take to offset the potentially permanent harm done to their property by taggers.

Beefing up the exterior lighting is one strategy. Another is to install physical deterrents, such as a fence or other landscaping element. Among the most widespread approaches fights fire with fire, so to speak.

Barrier coatings—a technical term for anti-graffiti paints—can be an effective ounce of prevention for masonry buildings, but choosing the correct formula is

critical. Some barrier coatings render repair and maintenance impossible. There are gloss-finish, water-soluble treatments that, depending on exposure to sun and wetness, may wear off in a few months; these are cheap fixes meant for situations where appearances don't matter. Other coatings—undetectable when applied, color stabilized, and dirt

The owners wanted an environment that reinforced their affinity for the simple, tactile technologies of the 19th century.

LEFT Because built-in bookcases wouldn't be at home in the quasi-industrial space, a more utilitarian arrangement was called for. A library system keeps the book collection organized and accessible. The hinged angle shelves display current reading materials and flip up to reveal additional storage behind.

repellent—are more appealing to the homeowner.

But should you come home one day to find that your uncoated door has been darkened by illegal urban expressionists, don't despair. Graffiti stripping—equal parts science and craft—is an option. Techniques for removal vary; popular methods include absorbent poultices, chemical strippers, and pressurized washing. Laser-based technologies are also being developed. All are best left to professionals, who are accomplished in analyzing the nature of both the stone and the stain—the wrong prescription can result in irreversible damage to the surface.

It's a field that's unfortunately overcrowded with underskilled practitioners. Local architectural preservation associations are a good source for referrals to competent service providers. Contacting officials working in museum conservation or restoration departments is another avenue that might yield leads to reputable contractors (or, just as important, warnings against unsatisfactory ones). In addition, many cities operate free or low-cost graffiti-removal programs; check with your local streets and sanitation department for help.

RECLAIMING A NEW YORK BROWNSTONE

DESIGN CHALLENGE > *to update the aesthetics of a brownstone duplex while respecting the remnants of the original structure*

When Jane and her husband, architect Arvid Klein, bought the brownstone on New York's Upper West Side, it had already undergone a number of significant changes (most of them not for the better) since it was erected in 1889 as a gracious single-family home. The most devastating change occurred at some point in the 1930s, when it was pressed into service as a rooming house; in the process of chopping it up into a dozen small apartments, the interior was stripped of most of its turn-of-the-century architectural character.

Before the couple bought the building, it belonged to another architect who had made some reparations to the house, converting it to a more habitable three units: a duplex and two floor-through resi-

OPPOSITE Partitions of vary-ing heights keep a space lively and open. The half-height wall here separates without being divisive; no kitchen clutter is visible, yet the cook isn't cut off from the action at the dining table.

RIGHT Back-to-back stretches of brownstones often conceal block-long swaths of surpris-ing lushness. While the gar-dens aren't common prop-erty, everyone can share in the verdant view.

dences. Jane and Arvid occupy the former, which comprises the ground floor and the one above it— what's known in brown-stone parlance as the parlor floor. The bedrooms and baths are downstairs, and the kitchen, living and din-ing areas, and a study are above them.

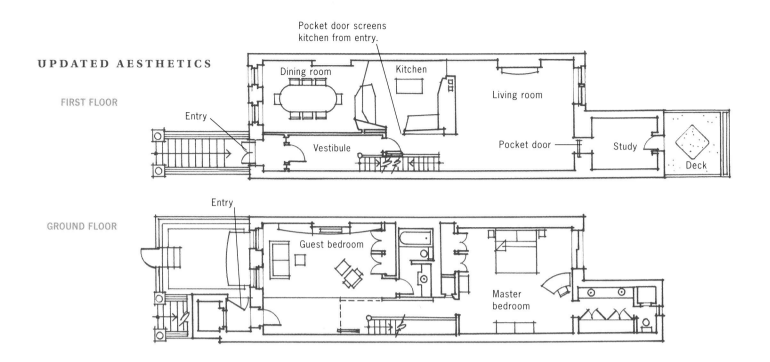

FIRST FLOOR

Pocket door screens
kitchen from entry.

Dining room

Kitchen

Living room

Entry

Vestibule

Pocket door

Study

Deck

GROUND FLOOR

Entry

Guest bedroom

Master
bedroom

RIGHT The balanced
proportions of turn-
of-the-century town
houses were often
destroyed when the
buildings were con-
verted into board-
ing houses. This
renovation recap-
tures the original
spatial integrity
and adapts it to
modern styles.

LEFT Whenever interior walls are erected, care must be taken not to impede the spread of light throughout the space. Cutting off the top of the kitchen enclosure and generous use of obscura glass ensure that adequate light levels are maintained.

THE HOUSE IS A WORK IN PROGRESS

How the Kleins redesigned their home is a tale shaped as much by ideas as objectives. Guided by both respect for the few surviving original details (the pocket door to the study, for one) as well as Arvid's modernist sensibility, the home is again a work in progress, its spaces undergoing subtle refinements and extensive renovation. Jane wryly points out that a dumpster has been a more or less steady presence out in front of the town house since they moved in.

In a nutshell, the design process is a deliberate, disciplined balancing of existing conditions, functional goals, and aesthetic expression. The kitchen is the most completely realized example of this process. It began with a thorough study of how the room is (and would be) used: storage capacities, sight lines, lighting priorities, and traffic patterns inside the kitchen as well as entering and exiting it.

ABOVE Putting every inch to work is especially important in compact areas where a variety of tasks are performed. Convenient open cubbies and closed storage help keep the kitchen organized.

ABOVE Keeping old features and giving them new functions is part of the evolution of city residences. In the dining room, the box of an obsolete fireplace was plastered over and now serves as an unconventional but convenient wine cellar.

A THOROUGHLY MODERN KITCHEN

Imagine a white gift box, almost a cube in form. One side has been cut away, and the lid is removed. Two of the remaining three top edges of the box have been trimmed down to about three-quarters of their original height; the third has been sliced even lower, maybe to half size. The lid has been flattened out into a square, colored a calming yellow, and moved off to the side, where it stands up against a wall.

This is the general configuration of Jane and Arvid's kitchen. It replaces one that was oriented east to west, which blocked the flow of light throughout the floor. Located between the living room and the dining area, it's well integrated into the floor plan, with one

The less-than-full height of the walls is a comfortable, contemporary compromise between an open kitchen and one that's enclosed.

entrance—a translucent-glass pocket door that, when closed, screens the sight of the kitchen from arriving visitors—convenient to the stair that leads to the front door.

The less-than-full height of the walls is a comfortable, contemporary compromise between an open kitchen and one that's enclosed. The shorter half-wall to the south lets the kitchen as well as the dining area bask in light from street-facing windows. On the far side of the kitchen, the wall stops just a couple of feet short of the 10-ft. 6-in. ceiling, forming a more substantial, formal border with the living room yet still allowing lots of sun to penetrate into the space. After dark, when the lights in the kitchen are switched on, an illuminated aura backlights the wall dramatically, showing off the sculptural quality of the kitchen structure.

In particular, the details and materials tell of the commitment Arvid, a principal with the firm Pasanella + Klein Stolzman + Berg, has to modernism as an evolving school of architecture. A compact trapezoidal work island, made of granite and perforated steel, edges the passage between the living and dining areas. Its irregular shape—not the revered modernist rectangle—along with the similarly clipped-off corners of the counters gives the geometry of the kitchen a playful, unexpected tweak.

The development of the study is more straightforward. In 1889, the space was a serving pantry, jutting off the then-dining room. By the time Jane and Arvid acquired the property, the first steps had been taken toward turning it into a full bath. Rather than carry this plan through to completion, however, the couple decided to put the abundant light and air enjoyed by the room to a more profitable use. They turned it into a study, which would

RIGHT Built-in furnishings preserve and sharpen a room's features that freestanding pieces would obscure and obstruct. Bookcases in the study reinforce its height; fixed shelves keep things orderly.

KEEPING COOL

In metropolitan areas, it's not just the nightlife that's hot. The temperatures in what climatologists call "urban heat islands" are typically 8 degrees to 10 degrees higher than surrounding settled areas, owing to the heat-retaining tendency of concrete and asphalt. Besides the sticky discomfort, energy costs hit homeowners in the pocket, and the accompanying plunge in air quality affects everyone.

Most people living in older buildings rely on in-window or through-the-wall air conditioners. In small, enclosed spaces, these can do the job just fine (assuming they're allowed; landmark buildings often have restricted usage).

Retrofitting a central air system is a formidable and expensive job, as Arvid and Jane would attest.

While air conditioning remains the method of choice for most to keep cool, there's a renewed appreciation for more environmentally sound solutions.

Low-tech approaches can definitely make a difference when the

be used far more frequently than a bathroom. They also added a squarish deck off this room, bringing a bit of outdoor life to the parlor floor.

BRINGING IN FRESH AIR

The most recent upgrade is invisible: a central air-conditioning system. Installing one of these in a vintage structure can be the stuff of urban legend, given the unique complexities of each site. Here, because the refrigerant couldn't handle the 50-ft. trip up to the roof, the condenser was sunk into an 8-ft.-deep well in the front of the building; putting it in the garden out back would have made the area intolerably noisy. It's a two-zone system: One air handler, in the cellar, feeds into the ground-floor spaces; the other is located in the study, where it cools the parlor floor.

ABOVE Paint and paper aren't the only ways to highlight wall surfaces—and they're not always up to the task in assertively architectural environments. Marble, granite, and mirrors in the master bath add heft and substance to the vertical plane in a measured but very effective application.

heat is on. Not only ecologically altruistic, the incentives are also economic. Something as simple as painting the roof a light-reflective color has been proven to significantly reduce the cost of cooling—annual savings of close to 20 percent isn't unheard of. And in Sacramento, California, there's a rebate offer in the works. Homeowners may receive up to 20 cents for every square foot of "cool roof" they install. It's worth noting that more than 50 roofing products are Energy Star–certified by the EPA, meaning they reflect at least 65 percent of the sun's rays when new and after three years' use a minimum of 50 percent.

There are even greener methods that are making inroads in several urban centers. At City Hall in Chicago, a $1.5 million, 20,000-sq.-ft. roof garden is taking root, in an experiment that's expected to yield $4,000 a year in lower air-conditioning costs. But progress in this area isn't confined to dollars saved; as ambient air temperatures go down, so do ozone levels—something everyone can breathe easy about.

SYLVAN SURPRISE

DESIGN CHALLENGE > *to transcend a derelict alley setting and create an attractive, welcoming home*

Whether it's viewed as inspiring, intimidating, or a seesawing combination of the two, living in the city taps into the resourcefulness of its residents. Enjoying no skyline view, no fashionable address, nor a king's-ransom budget, this house epitomizes that odds-beating spirit with a surplus of style, rising to the challenge to prove that it's possible to triumph over the ordinary—not to mention the marginal—building sites that are found throughout any metropolis.

COURTS AND GARDENS TRANSFORM INSIDE AND OUT

In neighborhoods where town houses dominate the streets, blocks are filled in with rectangular lots; there's a barracks-like regularity

RIGHT AND OPPOSITE More than skin deep, materials also work as metaphors. The view from the entrance encompasses an urban reference in the concrete block, while the rest of the space makes an overture to nature with its bright and airy volume, extensive use of woods, and focus on the garden.

to the pattern, if not the appearance, of the buildings that occupy them. It is in the core of such a section of Toronto that architects Brigitte Shim and Howard Sutcliffe designed their own home, one that goes against both the figurative grain and the literal grid of the norm.

LEFT Too often town houses simply sit passively on a site instead of engaging it. Here, rather than a straight, boring wall, recessing a back door along the side of the living room lets the interior reach out into the courtyard, locking the house and garden together.

SITED AGAINST THE GRAIN

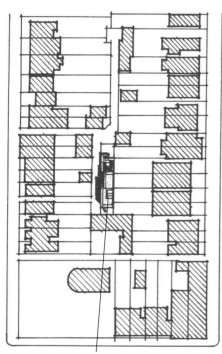

House sits on the block's
only north/south lot.

Even on paper the difference is evident. A look at the site plan of the house and its immediate vicinity (at left) provides a startling indication of just how much it contrasts with its context. The building sits on the block's only north/south lot, adjoining a service alley (which, in an apropos bit of urban irony, terminates in not one but two dead ends) where it's unceremoniously surrounded by the dowdy backsides of a dozen or so east/west-oriented parcels. A hot property with tremendous potential? Hardly.

What lifts the house above its scruffy milieu is the vision underlying its design. Rather than settling for being a bare-bones, utilitarian shelter, it was conceived of as a series of interior and exterior courts and gardens—a personal, pastoral slice of utopia.

Screening out the inarguably urban vista of junked cars, a concrete-block wall protects the house and its grounds. Seen from the alley, it seems as if nature is attempting to reclaim the site; a dense mass of vines trails over the wall, abetted by flowering plants and leafy trees. Like a long-lost ruin, the building, its boxy forms clad in stucco and wood, incongruously rises up from this jungle of a landscape.

Inside, it's apparent right away that the influence of the garden doesn't stop at the door. But the city itself does. It might as well be a world away, given the abundance of greenery. From the entry at a corner on the southern side of the house, there's a clear view through to the far end, where a wall-to-wall, floor-to-ceiling expanse of glass gives way to the courtyard. Designed with an awareness of the impact of the outdoors, the room doesn't attempt to compete with it, in form or finishes. The configuration of the interior is a direct reflection of the exterior: forthright rectangular volumes, organized in a line.

ABOVE Landscaping can play a powerful role in urban architecture—that of environmental equalizer. In large doses or small, greenery can take the rough edges off a vista that is less than spectacular and elevate it to something special.

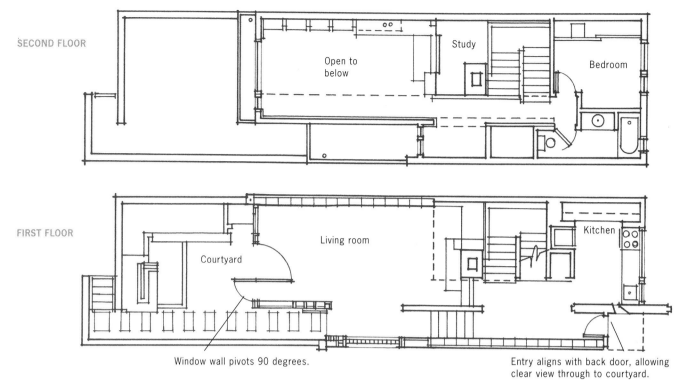

SECOND FLOOR

Open to below

Study

Bedroom

FIRST FLOOR

Courtyard

Living room

Kitchen

Window wall pivots 90 degrees.

Entry aligns with back door, allowing clear view through to courtyard.

ABOVE (LEFT AND RIGHT)
Architectural motifs tie the house together inside and out, upstairs and down. A blue wall stretches up from the ground level, pointing to the skylight, a translucent variation on the ceiling design of the lower floors.

HOME AS HIDEAWAY

The connections between the various spaces are broad and flowing, not truncated and abrupt like in an apartment nor centerless and without direction as in a raw, unrehabilitated loft. Such a plan is the logical response to the long, narrow site, as it seeks to maximize the amount of usable floor area in the house. The double height of the living/dining room also diverts attention from the slenderness of the space.

The floors are slate and Jatoba wood, striated in deep earthy colors. Concrete block and plaster work together on the walls, with a section of the gunmetal-blue wall rising up through the open stairwell to the second level. These materials carry through on the house's

LEFT A sense of intimacy can be cultivated, even in open spaces, through a concentration of visual elements. Colors and finishes mark five different wall planes in this alcove centered around a hearth, giving it a heightened sense of place.

concentrated connection with the garden, either as a direct extension of it or, in the case of the blue stairwell, as an abstraction of it. Continuity between the two stories is found in the ceiling design, with a board-and-batten treatment on the ground floor recalling the mullions of the skylight.

The best that most urbanites can hope for in terms of communing with nature from the comfort of their homes is usually limited to a clutch of potted plants arranged illegally on a fire escape or a kitchen herb garden perched on a windowsill. A lucky minority have balconies or terraces; fewer still have the privilege of roof decks or ground-level gardens. Brigitte and Howard's home surpasses each of these possibilities, a feat made all the more exceptional considering its uninspiring surroundings. And the relationship isn't restricted

RIGHT Windows are to see with and see through. In the kitchen, where a lot of competing cooking activities take place, large glazed panels help keep the emphasis on the outdoors as well as let in much-needed natural light.

SECURITY IN THE CITY

While a concrete-block wall is one answer to urban security concerns, a more focused and inclusive approach can be taken. For all types of residences—town houses, apartments, and lofts—doors are the points of entry most frequently targeted by burglars. Their technique of choice is still primarily brute force: kicking in the door or jimmying the lock. Experts advise homeowners to start with the standard, low-tech deterrents, beginning with a solid-core wood or steel door. It should be fitted with a 180-degree peephole and a quality dead bolt, with a minimum projection of ⅝ in. and a ¼-in.-dia. bolt. Go for a heavy-duty strike plate that's installed with 3-in. screws, instead of the usual 2½-in. ones (they're too short to grab into the sub-framing). Concealed fasteners and nonremovable hinge pins are also recommended.

These basics can be supplemented with a variety of electronic protection devices. Surveillance cameras can be hidden in smoke detectors or light fixtures. Motion detectors can be trained on portals, alerting occupants—as well as trespassers—with visual or audible alarms.

Unfortunately, a forced entry isn't the only way thieves gain access to a home. Too often they have a key. Your house is particu-

to a hands-off observation. The window wall can pivot a full 90 degrees, physically dissolving the already transparent barrier between indoors and the outside.

The garden—virtually a private park—takes a lesson from the home in its controlled use of texture and dimension. There are several principal elements that give it structure. A bank of raised concrete planters steps up and turns an inside corner within the walled enclosure, forming an L shape. Notched into the foot of the L is a fountain with a squared-off trough directing water into a small rectangular reflecting pool, the keystone that holds this tight little composition together.

LEFT AND BELOW Security and aesthetics can happily coexist. As the wall surrounds the garden, the garden surrounds the house, simultaneously protecting the property and bringing beauty to the neighborhood.

larly vulnerable when there's renovation work going on, and it's necessary to have an unsupervised parade of tradespeople coming and going. Utilizing multiple personalized codes that can be regularly changed, electronic key-tracking systems can be configured to limit authorized entrances. Right now, such systems are expensive, but when weighed against potential losses, they may merit the investment.

BRIDGING PAST AND PRESENT

DESIGN CHALLENGE > *to restore the exterior to its original condition while opening up the interior for a modern feel*

RIGHT Behind these brownstone walls is a revitalized interior, planned to respond to modern living patterns.

OPPOSITE In the new, free-flowing floor plan, the kitchen bridges the dining and living areas. The stair leads up to the master suite and down to the garden level. Open risers and railings lessen its intrusion into the room and promote the flow of light between floors.

The renovation of this 1891 brownstone posed an architectural paradox of time and space. On the exterior, architects Marsella & Knoetgen's job was to take the building back to the 19th century, restoring the facade to its former condition. But on the interior, time would flow in the opposite direction. Homeowners Caitlin and Brendan wanted a lofty, open floor plan with a modern feel.

The town house is in a historic-landmark district, which meant that any work done on the street side of the building was subject to close scrutiny and review by a local approval committee—above and beyond the normal building codes. To realize their clients' goals, the architects had to undo the mistakes of the past to a set of strict criteria. The guidelines, based on maintaining the uniform appearance of the neighborhood's brownstones, were exacting, specifying such minute details as the dimensions of the new window frames (they had to measure within ¼ in. of those of the existing windows) and the acceptable design for the front stair.

RIGHT Older buildings make challenging candidates for stylistic renovation. In this New York City brownstone, the transformation is first noticeable in the vestibule, where the wainscoting is distinctly contemporary.

BELOW Built-in features help to update a period interior. Sleek new cherry wood accents—a service bar and wine rack—and cased openings do the trick here.

AN OPEN FLOOR PLAN TRANSFORMS THE INTERIOR

Inside, the first order of business was to rip out the quartet of small apartments that spatially strangled the first two floors of the building. Constructed in the first part of the 1900s, well before any pride of place sensibility took root in the area, this earlier remodel had essentially scuttled the original interior; most of the decorative moldings and millwork were lost. Out on the street, the brownstone's artfully carved stone stoop—a mainstay of New York's sidewalk social life—had also disappeared.

Landmark restrictions need to be factored in to some designs. The tall street-side windows are the only remaining hint of the home's turn-of-the century origins. Otherwise, it's been transformed into a thoroughly modern residence in plan and detailing.

An existing staircase that serviced the now-vanquished apartments—and continues to do so for the remaining tenants, who occupy homes on the other floors—could not be moved. Because it runs through the couple's apartment on the east wall, the general layout of the first floor was designed around it. As a result, the first-floor plan has a slight C shape to it.

A new set of stairs that wouldn't be used by any of the brownstone's other residents had to be built for Brendan and Caitlin's home, to connect their levels of living space. Committed to minimizing its impact on the space, it was decided that the stair should be located away from the front of the house and parallel with the bearing walls; otherwise, it would interrupt the open plan of the main floor. Stacking it on top of the stairs that run down to the garden level further conserves floor space. More than a vehicle for circulation, the stair slips through generous openings in the ceilings, which let a shaft of light fall from the floor above. Open railings and risers facili-

BELOW Thoughtful detailing can significantly affect the impression made by an interior. Throughout the first floor, a narrow reveal runs between the ceiling and the walls, a gallery-like touch that unifies the space. Windows on the back of the building were enlarged, reaching down to the floor.

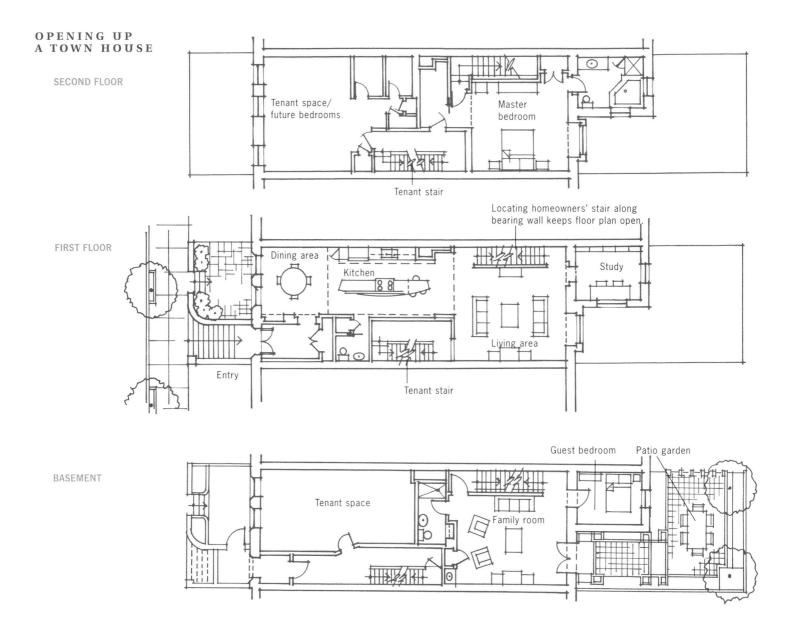

SECOND FLOOR

Tenant space/
future bedrooms

Master
bedroom

Tenant stair

Locating homeowners' stair along
bearing wall keeps floor plan open.

FIRST FLOOR

Dining area

Kitchen

Study

Living area

Entry

Tenant stair

BASEMENT

Guest bedroom   Patio garden

Tenant space

Family room

RIGHT Ground-level
gardens extend
living space.
Brendan and
Caitlin's patio is
reached through
the family room.

LEFT Long and narrow open spaces need a resting point to prevent town-house tunnel syndrome. With its bowfront shape, this kitchen island throws a curve into the elongated floor plan. A collage of steel, glass, granite, and maple, it's also the material focus of the home.

tate its spread into the core of the interior, where it brightens areas that are too far from windows to enjoy much sun. Subdued colors, construction, and materials work to keep the stair a quiet presence.

AN EYE-CATCHING KITCHEN
IS THE FOCUS OF THE HOME

The show-stopping element was reserved for the kitchen, which is situated in the middle of the narrow floor between the dining and living areas. This location saves the windows at either end of the floor for the social spaces. A wall of glass-fronted, honey-colored cabinets forms a backdrop for the cooking island, itself a concentrated display of geometry. A sculptural intersection of vertical, horizontal, and

BELOW Interior shutters, with one panel fixed and one louvered, allow the option of light and view or shade and privacy. The louvered panel can be adjusted to filter sunlight in or out.

curving planes, it supplies a centralized location for casual dining, cooking, and kitchen storage. The island is also the material epicenter of the residence, combining maple, stainless steel, glass, and granite into one eye-catching composition. The rest of the town house is purposely kept neutral in anticipation of additions to Brendan and Caitlin's growing art collection.

SEEING THE LIGHT

A common problem in row houses like Caitlin and Brendan's is how to brighten up the dark midpoint of the building's lower floors; even after enlarging the windows, daylight doesn't fully reach into the space. Knowing a few artificial-lighting basics can go a long way toward alleviating a shadowy situation.

An effective lighting plan combines the three fundamental types of illumination: ambient, or general, lighting; task lighting; and accent, or feature, lighting.

Ambient lighting simulates daylight by providing an even distribution of brightness throughout a room, usually by using overhead fixtures such as chandeliers,

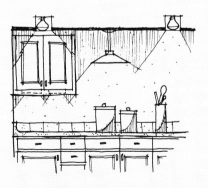

recessed lights, or track lights. It forms the foundation of all lighting schemes and can be supplemented by the following two types.

An earlier remodel had essentially scuttled the original interior; most of the decorative moldings and millwork were lost.

BELOW City archives and historical associations can often be of assistance in restoration projects. Here, photos dating from the 1930s provided visual clues for reconstructing the front stairs.

The renovation includes a new powder room on the main floor. Constructed in an alcove next to the kitchen pantry, it doesn't interrupt the flow of space and saves a trip up or down the stairs. Closed off by a cherry-framed pocket door, inset with panes of etched glass, its design echoes that of the island.

RECONSTRUCTING THE STONE STOOP

The architects tracked down some photographs taken for a tax assessment in the 1930s and used them as a model for recreating the graceful entry stoop. A slight snag in the job occurred with the bas-relief panel at the bottom of the stair. In their original submission, Marsella & Knoetgen had sketched a symmetrical detail for the carving, which the landmarks commission found acceptable. When the design was later changed to a traditional, albeit asymmetrical, Celtic-knot pattern, it was necessary to reapply for approval. To achieve the required balanced composition, the motif had to be manipulated: a mirror image was created and centered. Permission granted.

Task lighting, not surprisingly, is focused on a specific function: reading, grooming, cooking, or what-have-you. Fixtures should be selected to support the task in question. Pendant lights, portable lamps, and undershelf designs are examples. Most important, it should be glare- and shadow-free; careful positioning of the fixtures is key to those qualities.

Accent lighting highlights specific objects or features in a room. It should be at least three times as bright as the ambient light in a space and is typically provided by track, recessed, or wall-mounted fixtures.

In addition to the array of fixtures to choose from, there are controls and lamps to be considered. Dimmer switches let you alter the mood of a room. Timers or motion sensors can improve energy efficiency and enhance a home's security.

Light-source technology is ever advancing. A new breed of compact fluorescent lamps greatly improves upon earlier models and is making inroads into what had been the exclusive territory of the traditional incandescent bulb. Their light color and quality equals those of incandescents, they're buzz- and flicker-free, and they excel at conserving energy. For under-cabinet lighting, halogen has always been a popular choice, but it burns hot; cool, long-lasting xenon bulbs are an emerging alternative.

TOWN-HOUSE RENOVATION
PASSES THE TEST OF TIMES

DESIGN CHALLENGE > *to accommodate the contemporary needs of a young family while respecting the historic context of a turn-of-the century home*

Hiking through the city, it's easy to appreciate how different eras put their own stamp on the look of the metropolis. Dissimilar architectures mingle without acrimony, the dense context of the street absorbing the new alongside the old. It's possible to traverse a cross-section of design history in the course of a single block: A variety of period building styles interspersed with glossy modern edifices can be an absorbing discovery. But to encounter a collage of this nature on the *inside* of a building—even most unlikely, a residential one—is an unusual event indeed. In the renovation of this Chicago town house for a growing family, the firm of Morgante-Wilson embarked on a bit of playful architectural time traveling.

OPPOSITE Sometimes it's a variety of focused details, rather than a repeating theme, that gives definition and meaning to an interior. For example, in this home the parade of different columns is a chronology of style and technology that begins with carved wooden pilasters by the front door and concludes with steel I-beams bracing the bottom of the lightwell.

LEFT Many urban neighborhood organizations severely restrict alterations to the front facades of residential structures, even if they do not have landmark status. This often leaves the back of a building fair game for artistic expression, a canvas on which to continue the work within.

FIRST FLOOR

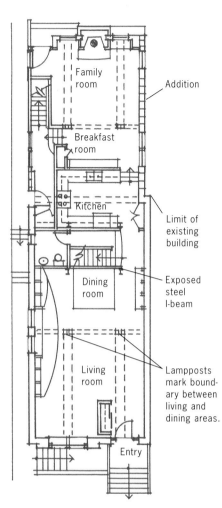

Family room

Addition

Breakfast room

Limit of existing building

Kitchen

Exposed steel I-beam

Dining room

Living room

Lampposts mark boundary between living and dining areas.

Entry

SECOND FLOOR

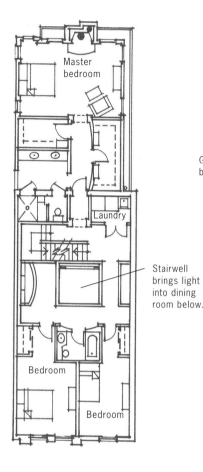

Master bedroom

Laundry

Stairwell brings light into dining room below.

Bedroom

Bedroom

THIRD FLOOR

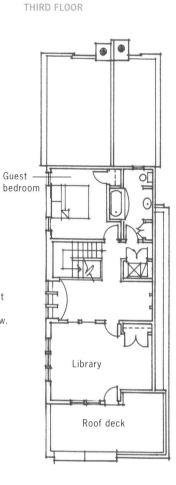

Guest bedroom

Library

Roof deck

ABOVE While it's usually more economical to expand outward rather than upward, the real gain to city dwellers is measured not in dollars but in square footage. Half of the kitchen, the breakfast area, and the family room comprise this addition at ground level.

NEW MEETS OLD

The original building was a solid structure dating from the 1880s, built out of brick with pink sandstone lintels and decorative banding in the then-popular Victorian fashion. At some time over the last 30 years, the building was broken up into three apartments. To allow the creation of an adventurous yet family-friendly floor plan, the building was gutted as a first step toward establishing a relaxed mix of open and enclosed spaces. On the ground level, the living and dining areas flow into one another, as do the breakfast and family rooms in the back of the house. Spaces on the two upper floors are more conventionally contained, in keeping with their capacities as bedrooms and a library.

The remodeling returns the building to its origin as a single-family home and expands upon it with a 3,100-sq.-ft. addition tacked onto the rear of the house. Not only are the existing house and the addition linked together physically but symbolically as well. As the structural components and finish details progress through the house from front to back and bottom to top, the language of the architec-

ABOVE With the costs of a competent restoration often exceeding those of a complete remodel, many older buildings have contemporary interiors. Upstairs, this master bedroom is the antithesis of Victorian space. Bright, clean-lined, and airy, it's the anchor to a suite retreat that includes his-and-hers walk-in closets and an ample master bath.

LEFT It's possible to define discrete spaces without relying on walls. A steel framework plays both functional and decorative roles as it forms an open-sided pavilion for the dining area.

ABOVE Solid banks of cabinetry—even those fronted with visually lightening glass doors—can make a kitchen feel oppressive as well as impede the flow of light into the room. This design solves these problems by floating cabinets over the counter, and the open grid of shelving topping them helps convey light from the western windows into the space.

ture becomes incrementally more contemporary. Just beyond the front door is the "oldest" part of the house, while the upstairs room overlooking the backyard—it happens to be the master bedroom—is rendered in the most up-to-date fashion. It's a subtle way of enlivening and unifying the interior that doesn't stifle with sameness.

FOLLOW THE COLUMNS TO DATE THE HOUSE

The street-facing facade was left unchanged; the transitional experiences begin when you step inside. The clues to the chronology are in the various types of columns used throughout the town house. Immediately edging the door are wooden pilasters, faithful to the millwork of the era when the house was constructed. Walking straight ahead, the next architectural indicators appear. Two pairs of slender, ornamental cast-iron Victorian lampposts mark the boundary between the living and dining areas. The uprights would normally culminate in glass globes; obviously, under these load-bearing circumstances, something sturdier was called for.

In response, Morgante-Wilson created a fresh turn on the column capital. Small trapezoidal flanges were welded together, their flared tops supporting overhead girders. On the far side of the dining room (going farther back in space and time, if you will), the columns were pared down to a minimal presence: Steel I-beams stand exposed and sculptural. Moving past the stair to the kitchen, metal beams skim in and out of vertical wedges of drywall in a final, postmodern evolution of the column.

Exiting the house through the back door, it's revealed that the mix-to-match attitude of the renovation continues. The rear facade combines two elements—one brick, the other white clapboard—into a dynamic composition. The wood siding covers about three quadrants of the elevation (roughly from nine o'clock to six o'clock), with the masonry facing the ground-floor family room and rising to form the chimneys. It's the point where the design map originally sketched out for the project culminates: Two traditional, true-to-context materials are used in a thoroughly contemporary fashion.

ABOVE In many urban homes, stairs are seen as space wasters, little more than a necessary evil in an environment where every inch counts. When there's more room to work with, though, as in this town house, the stairway can become an architectural event, dramatically lit and detailed—a focal point in its own right.

WORKING WITH COLUMNS

Columns are an integral part of the structure of several urban building types and are expressed in different ways.

Warehouses and factories suitable for residential conversions are normally filled with a grid of freestanding columns. Whatever their form and material—massive wooden timbers, concrete mushrooms, or cast-iron piers—all help maximize the amount of open space. When individual loft units are enclosed, a "connect the dots" approach is typically taken to the floor plan, using the columns as guideposts to the construction of dividing walls. While the pillars weren't originally intended to be objects of beauty, when left exposed they lend architectural authenticity to the spaces that's worth retaining. Some building codes may require columns to be sheathed in fire-rated materials; check on this regulation before stripping (or wrapping) them.

In high-rises, columns are often part of the exterior walls, insensitively bumping out into the living areas. If leaving columns in their natural state isn't a viable aes-

RIGHT Architecture doesn't have to be confined to quarters; bringing elements of it outdoors gives a unifying feel to the entire home. Here, some of the geometric motifs begun inside the home continue to find a place in the design of the elements of the backyard: the circular patio, the arcing stairs, and the bench.

THE CHALLENGE OF THE OLD

When working with older structures, it's fairly predictable that there will be a few challenges that will crop up during construction. In worst-case scenarios, these are invisible and undocumented conditions that have far-reaching (i.e., expensive) implications on the timely completion of the job. Fortunately, with this home, these issues could be identified early on and were addressed in the design phase of the project. One of the difficulties was how to insert a new structural system into the existing masonry shell without jeopardizing the integrity of the walls. Extensive bracing was put into place before removing the structural components of the original house; new truss joists were then installed to achieve a clear 20-ft. span in the interior.

Another problem was coping with limited access to the backyard when excavating and constructing the addition. As with many sites in the city occupied by buildings from decades past, properties were built all the way out to the lot lines, allowing very little room for digging the foundation and erecting walls. The crumbly, sandy soil only complicated the situation further. So the job—and the budget—had to expand to include shoring up the neighbors' homes.

The clues to the chronology are in the various types of columns used throughout the town house.

thetic option, there are some things to consider when developing a covering for them. Integrating an obtrusive object into the overall design of a space is tricky business. Taking cues from other elements in the home—following the proportions of cabinetry, fenestration patterns, and door openings—can form the basis of providing a cogent solution to the ugly-column conundrum.

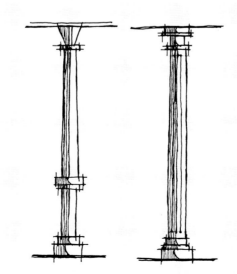

LIVING ON THE LEVELS

DESIGN CHALLENGE > *to*

develop an innovative,
design-conscious model
for infill housing

For an architect, creating a home of one's own is very different than designing one for a client. With a commissioned project, there's an objective agenda (e.g., three bedrooms, a fully wired home office, a kitchen that accommodates two cooks), and in most cases, the way those needs are fulfilled is in a straightforward, functional manner. While the same pragmatic planning is no less true for the architect/ homeowner, there's often a greater willingness to treat the building process, as well as its form, more as an experiment. In this Montreal duplex, the design/construction firm Build did just that, exploring the melding of style and shelter while investigating the larger possibilities of efficient and imaginative infill design.

OPPOSITE Infill structures usually have windows only on the front and back sides of the building, making it difficult to brighten the heart of the interior. Keeping the vertical circulation core as transparent as possible, with minimal metal railings and open stair treads, lets light flow unimpeded through the space.

THINKING THIN

Located in the Plateau Mont-Royal part of town, the house intentionally upsets the typical arrangement of individual apartments stacked on top of one another. Instead, the structure is split down the middle, with each of the two side-by-side units having access to the street and to a rear garden. One of the units is home to a couple of Build's principals, Danita Rooyakkers and Attila Tolnai.

What makes this vertical division all the more interesting are the dimensions of the project. The vacant lot measures 23½ ft. wide by 86 ft. long; each residence rises to 35 ft., extends 56 ft. into the

SIX-FLOOR CROSS SECTION

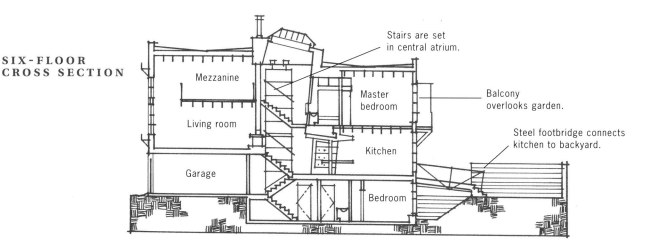

Mezzanine

Living room

Garage

Stairs are set in central atrium.

Master bedroom

Kitchen

Bedroom

Balcony overlooks garden.

Steel footbridge connects kitchen to backyard.

property, and is a sliverlike 10 ft. 8 in. wide. Floor plans for the thin twins are the mirror opposite of each other and provide approximately 1,600 sq. ft. of habitable space, spread out over six levels.

When seen from the street, though, the building belies that reality; because of the way the windows are configured, it seems to have just two stories, the same as the neighboring structures. A mix of bricks and concrete block continues the masonry construction that characterizes the facades in the immediate vicinity. While the materials are compatible with its context, the duplex's appearance is distinct from it. The architects have injected an unmistakably industrial flavor into the town house, with a cornice made of folded metal and the back of the building sheathed in corrugated metal siding.

In response to the city mandate requiring on-site parking, the Build team developed a novel, flexible solution that's sure to appeal to city dwellers who don't own cars while appeasing the building department. On the ground floor, three glass-fronted doors are grouped together. One of them can swing wide to admit a person, or

LEFT AND BELOW Narrow homes—this one measures only 10 ft. 8 in. wide—don't have room to waste on interior walls. Steel-framed panels of corrugated plastic are suspended in the middle of the stairwell, providing an anchorage for the handrail without consuming space or blocking light.

in conjunction with the other two doors (bifold models that can be pushed off to the side), all three can be opened to accommodate a vehicle. The space inside, it follows, can be utilized either as a garage or as a studio or workshop, a win/win situation for drivers and public-transit riders alike.

CENTRAL STAIR CONNECTS SIX STAGGERED LEVELS

Once inside, visitors face a choice: follow a half-flight of stairs up or down. The decision is one that recurs four times in the house, as the steps zig and zag to connect the six staggered levels. In tandem with clever window sizing and placement, floating the floors—specifically, the mezzanine—around the stairs also facilitates the two-story illusion on the exterior. Hanging from the top of the building, a series of clear corrugated plastic panels stretches through the middle of the stairwell, a transparent core that carries through on the promise of the skylight overhead as well as the constellations of little halogen spotlights that illuminate the stairs at night.

LEFT Sight lines in city homes are most typically trained on internal views. Here, in marked contrast to the scene at the other end of the kitchen, the organization of the home is in focus, with the floor levels giving the impression of floating in space. The cantilevered kitchen island echoes this aspect of the structure.

LIVING SPACES IN BACK OPEN TO OUTSIDE

The back half of the home is devoted to personal living spaces. To varying extents, each one of these floors has a link to the outdoors. On the ground level (actually, it's a little below grade), a bath/bedroom suite has access to a backyard patio; two levels up is the master suite, where a balcony looks out onto the rear garden. Sandwiched between them is the kitchen, which has a most interesting connection to the backyard: a steel footbridge. Befitting the narrow floor plan, the area is laid out as a galley, with refrigerator, cooktop, oven, sink, and dishwasher spread along one wall. Across the room stand a table and chairs. Incorporating the dining area into the kitchen frees up valuable space elsewhere in the home and suits the slightly raw quality that's fostered by touches such as exposed joists and metal siding.

By necessity, storage assumes some ingenious forms throughout the house. A bank of large, deep closets lines the stairwell just below the kitchen. In the master bedroom and bath, sliding maple

LEFT The quest to integrate nature into city living is ceaseless. A great opportunity posed by the diminutive dimensions of these quarters is seized: A glazed wall is created at the rear of the home using standard-size windows, giving diners a pleasant garden vista.

Incorporating the dining area into the kitchen frees up valuable space elsewhere in the home.

panels conceal cupboards in the upper register of the 12-ft.-tall walls. Several rooms lacking that height feature small 24-in. cabinets as part of their entries, supplementing standard 72-in. closets.

PUBLIC SPACES FACE THE STREET

Public spaces are stacked along the front of the home. Near the tall windows on the street-side wall, the living room capitalizes on the height of the building, with the ceiling opening up to nearly 20 ft. This accommodates the uppermost level in the home, a mezzanine, which is suspended over the living room to within about 8 ft. of the front wall of the building. It can be used for any number of purposes where visual privacy and a large floor area aren't major concerns: an office, a library, a playroom, or even a nursery. This kind of functional flexibility can be refined and recycled into other residences—Build is looking to inform and inspire urban planners and developers about alternative concepts for infill designs—a progressive result of using a house as a laboratory for ideas.

A CHOICE OF STAIRS

Verticality is the quintessential characteristic of urban living, as borne out by the vital role played by stairs in this Montreal house. Choosing a stair configuration is to some extent determined by the local building code, which differs from city to city. Headroom clearance, the height of risers, the depth of treads, and the area and intervals of landings—all are prescribed by the authorities (frequently in terms of minimum/ maximum limits). By adhering to these guidelines while taking into account the architectural conditions, a custom design can be created.

There are three basic types of stair layouts, each offering its own aesthetic as well as practical appeal. As a matter of safety, all should be well lighted, with an easy-to-grip handrail and slip-resistant treads.

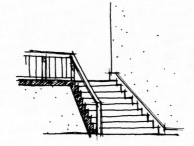

Straight-run stairs. The simplest style to build, they are also the greediest when it comes to floor area, typically occupying a 3-ft. by 12-ft. footprint. They do, however, lend themselves to some jazzy, city-suitable interpretations: a cantilevered design or

LEFT When one dimension of a building is restricted, the others can often be optimized. This slender residence runs 56 ft. deep and stands 35 ft. tall. Six staggered floor levels are connected by five flights of stairs, which are set in a central atrium. Here, the flue of the wood stove follows the vertical volume of the upper half of the home.

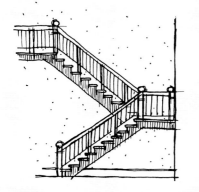

a single, central stringer. Such variations call for a structural engineer's attention.

L- and U-shaped stairs. These are short runs of straight stairs that are connected by at least one land-ing, at which point the stair reverses direction in a kind of switchback path. These don't need the floor area required by a single run of stairs. The stairway in the Montreal house is U-shaped in plan.

Spiral stairs. This is the most space-saving design but also poses the most user restrictions. A curved stair can be difficult to navigate for young and old, and a tight radius may limit the stair's usefulness when trying to haul things up and down. For those reasons, many building

departments discourage spirals. On the other hand, they're undeniably eye-catching and are readily available in cost-effective kits or as prefab subassemblies, which are often used to provide access to sleeping lofts.

PRESERVING INDEPENDENCE

DESIGN CHALLENGE > *to re-model for wheelchair accessibility while maintaining the historic character of the building and garden area*

OPPOSITE In neighborhoods with historic-landmark status, renovations—if allowed at all—are rarely permitted to be visible from the street. The addition to this Philadelphia "trinity house" is off the back of the building.

Philadelphia has no shortage of picturesque, antique buildings lining its cobbled alleyways. Connie and Norman, looking to move back to the city, succumbed to their appeal and purchased a pair of "trinity houses" to be enjoyed as their retirement home. The petite brick row structures have a unique floor plan: A single room occupies each of their three stories (including a basement level), which is how they get their name. When Norman, in the aftermath of a stroke, began to use a wheelchair, the tiny homes had to be adapted to accommodate his changed needs.

Zoning ordinances wouldn't allow the common wall separating the two buildings to be opened up to create a continuous first floor. And the homeowners' passion for historic preservation precluded accessibility features that they thought would intrude on the integrity of their home. Elevator lifts, pipe railings, and other overt means of assistance were rejected as too clinical, incompatible with the trinities' carefully maintained early-18th-century ambience.

Connie and Norman were also determined to protect the charming garden off the back of the buildings. Besides being an attractive landscape, the garden would have to serve as the pathway Norman would use to reach the other house—so a full-size addition was out of the question. Combined, these criteria presented an unusually challenging assignment to architect James Oleg Kruhly.

ABOVE Sensitive remodelings strive to enhance, not disturb, the original character of the house. This 18th-century home has an unexpected delicacy of form.

WHEN DOORS CLOSE, SPACE OPENS

Because the house was so compact, a well-organized plan was crucial to the project, and the bathroom, having the greatest number of complicated building-code requirements to fulfill, quickly became the key to the design. Working through several variations, Kruhly found one configuration that functioned well without consuming a lot of the already limited space or ignoring the distinctive qualities of the original architecture. He broke the bath into two separate enclosures, on opposite walls from one another. One contains the shower; the other houses the water closet and lavatory.

The space between the enclosures is critical: It's sized to allow Norman to maneuver freely through the house. When the doors to both bathroom facilities are closed, a passageway is created between the new sitting room/library addition (in the rear) and the street-side bedroom. When the doors are open a full 90 degrees, the doors can be locked together, screening the sitting room from the baths and beyond. A separate set of folding doors closes off the view from the street.

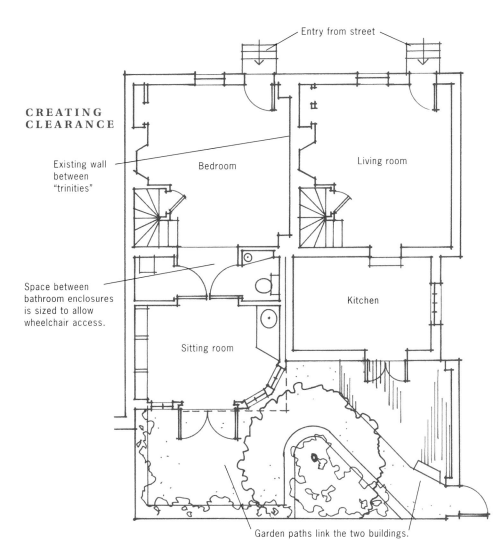

CREATING CLEARANCE

Entry from street

Existing wall between "trinities"

Bedroom

Living room

Space between bathroom enclosures is sized to allow wheelchair access.

Sitting room

Kitchen

Garden paths link the two buildings.

The space between the enclosures is critical: It's sized to allow the home-owner to maneuver freely through the house.

ABOVE A house that's just two rooms deep needs some provisions for privacy. The doors to the baths swing open and close off the rooms.

ABOVE To conserve floor area, the bath facilities were split over two enclosures. The shower features built-in seating.

ABOVE Joining new architecture to old is a delicate operation. Working with accessibility codes makes it more so. The width of the passageway accommodates the turning radius of Norman's wheelchair and complements the house's 18th-century proportions. Note the smooth transition in floor materials—no bumpy threshold.

PRESENT MEETS PAST

With its mullioned glass walls and French doors, the sitting room has the strong connections to the garden that the homeowners wanted. Quarry tiles measuring 8 in. by 8 in. cover the floor, alluding to the paved patio outside. A dormer adds height to the room, and a light-well carved out of the ceiling delivers sun into the middle of the space and invites an even larger part of the ivy-covered garden wall inside. All these ingredients—transparency, natural light, and vertical space—team together to belie the smallness of the room, which measures just 6 ft. by 9 ft. For convenience, a sink, microwave, and under-counter refrigerator are tucked into a corner of the room. (A new, fully furbished kitchen that's used by Norman's live-in aide is located on the first level of the trinity. The aide's sleeping quarters are up on the third floor.)

The addition is wrapped in wood siding, making it friendly with the renovation of the partner trinity, a job done years before Norman and Connie took over the property. Multipaned windows and doors, all topped with transoms, are compatible with a broad reading of

OPPOSITE Light, height, and views of the outdoors make small spaces feel larger. All three elements are at work in the new sitting room.

ABOVE It's impossible to ignore the house next door when it has a wall in common. The clapboard was influenced by the siding of the addition to the adjacent house, which was done many years before the sitting room was built. The angled wall directs the flow of space.

period style. The composition and mass of the addition, though, breaks away from the flat planes and quiet, stolid austerity of the Federalist period, adding a spirited twist to the facade. Clipping the corner of the sitting room nearest the adjoining building is a neighborly gesture, one house cozying up to the other. It also affords a more inclusive view of the garden.

The backyard has been altered and updated for Norman's use, done with great care to preserve the lush rusticity—so precious in the city—that makes the setting special. Low walls of dry-stacked stone edge the planting beds and ramps. Unobtrusively paved in red common Philadelphia brick, the inclined paths run through the garden, linking the trinities. It's an example of an uncommon architecture, providing access to the present by literally going through the past.

UNIVERSAL DESIGN

When building a large-scale project like this remodeling in Philadelphia, it's best to work with an architect who's knowledgeable about the standards for barrier-free construction. Whether it's motorized or staggered counter heights, specialized lighting schemes, or automated home systems, an experienced architect will be able to tailor the environment to the special needs of the user.

But there are plenty of incidental, around-the-house upgrades that can be made without professional help. Implementing them in a home or apartment isn't a reflection on age or ability; universal design (UD) is meant to make life easier for everyone. Almost anyone who's moderately handy with a screwdriver can make these improvements:

- Put lever-style handles on doors and faucets.

- Install adjustable-height or handheld shower fixtures.

- Use rocker-panel light switches.

- Attach loop or D-shaped pulls to cabinets.

- Lay textured, nonslip flooring in the bath.

Some UD modifications that would require a licensed tradesperson include:

■ Move electrical outlets up to at least 27 in. off the floor, and lower light switches to between 44 in. and 48 in. off the floor.

■ Install anti-scald plumbing controls in the bath.

■ Install hands-free faucets.

■ Mount fixed or flip-up seating in the shower.

■ Outfit kitchen and bath cabinetry with roll-out shelves or trays.

Particularly as the aging-in-place trend increases—the Miliken Institute reports that most of America's 78 million baby boomers will retire in the metropolitan areas where they spent their peak career years, rather than the traditional sun spots like Florida and Arizona—applying universal design principles is a sound investment for city dwellers.

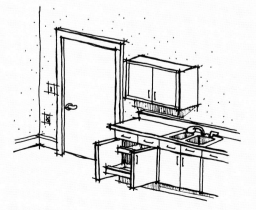

CAPITOL GAINS

DESIGN CHALLENGE > *to join the owner's existing home and a neighboring property and provide access to a garden*

OPPOSITE Especially in small confines, contrasting spaces add interest to an environment; there's always a compelling destination within the home. Here, the snug bedroom is a retreat from the double-height area off the garden and the open, floating platform of the annex's second-level living area.

In the Capitol Hill section of Washington, D.C., there's an enclave of houses whose organization reflects the urban block structure of centuries gone by. An array of stately, spacious town houses fronts the main street, with tidy, painted-brick row houses tucked behind them, facing a court or service alley. Originally these long, narrow homes were used by workers, and over the years they've developed a particular charm.

David, a media producer, had been living comfortably in one of these houses for more than 10 years, undaunted by its 14-ft. by 44-ft. size. Still, when an adjacent alley home came on the market, he did not pass up the opportunity to acquire it. Not that annexing another building would drastically increase his living space—the two-story neighbor measures a mere 11 ft. by 30 ft.—but it had what so many city residents yearn for: a small, private garden. The outside area was made all the more desirable because his current home fully occupied its lot, right up to the property lines. He called on McInturff Architects to negotiate the architectural merger.

The project could afford to be more adventuresome and open-ended than most remodelings because David had no rigid requirements or pressing concerns about how the new half of his home should be utilized (except to provide a sprinkling of vantage points from which to contemplate the garden). As a result, the architects

enjoyed an inordinate amount of conceptual freedom. In the end, the aim of all parties was to create a spectrum of spatial experiences, ranging from the intimate to the theatrical. But while the individual environments may differ within the new part of the home, there's an overall feeling of serenity pervading it.

BREAKING DOWN THE WALLS

The job began by wiping the slate clean: All the interior walls, floors, and ceilings were gutted in the new house. The front and back walls were furred out to conceal mechanical chases, then plastered and painted. The side walls were kept as exposed brick and painted white. Because the two buildings share a common wall, joining them was a relatively simple act of deconstruction. Breaking down the masonry divider gave the ground floor of the original building access to the garden. Upstairs, the new room supplied overflow seating for the existing living area. (As far as a transitional space is concerned, there is none: The original home, with its postmodern pale colors and sharply delineated geometry was not included in the renovation.) The lateral expansion accomplished, the stage was set for developing the vertical space.

ABOVE When two buildings are made one, both structure and style issues come to the fore, begging for resolution. In this D.C. town house, it was decided to let the character of the original building stay as is and to treat the new attachment independently.

OPPOSITE A priority for the homeowner was to create multiple observation points that focused on the rear garden. The old home now affords several views out to it, including a balcony on the upper floor and an ample opening on the ground level.

FIRST FLOOR

SECOND FLOOR

Wall opening
marks transition
between origi-
nal house and
new annex.

Courtyard

Window
wall

Living
room

Master
bedroom

Entry

ORIGINAL
HOME

NEW
ANNEX

Balcony

Sitting
room

Built-in
benches

ORIGINAL
HOME

NEW
ANNEX

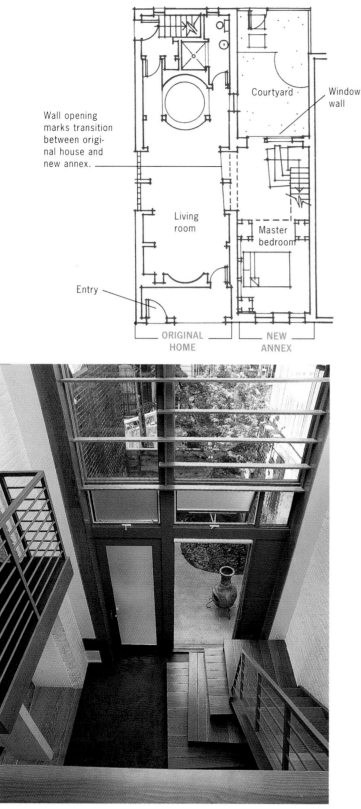

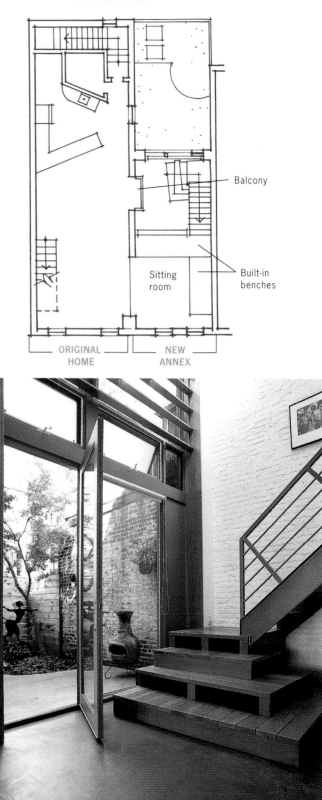

ABOVE Visually or physically, incorporating nature into an urban home provides a sanctuary from the surrounding bustle. A two-story window wall lets
the garden of this D.C. row house be appreciated from two perspectives:
the mezzanine and ground level.

ABOVE Architectural continuity needn't stop inside the home; where possible,
extending details outdoors brings a sense of completion to the project. A
cedar fence carries the wood treatment from the front wall of the annex to
the back wall of the garden.

DEVELOPING THE SPACE, WITH AN ACCENT ON WOOD

To make the most of the long-absent link to the outdoors, the rear wall of the annex is almost entirely glazed, with a glass door leading to the fenced-in courtyard. The window wall floods the double-height space with light; horizontal fir louvers help to cut down on the glare and add a bit of privacy.

Wood is the principal material in the new interior, a complement to the whitewashed brick walls. A stair ascends along one side of the room, its first four steps foreshadowing the spare design of the second floor. A stack of square, pallet-like platforms, the steps decrease in size as they rise, until they meet the straight run of stairs. On reaching the upper level, low-slung, built-in benches edge the room on two sides; even the wood floor is slightly elevated, all continuing the elemental construction of the steps. Each of these planes

ABOVE Openness is an asset in tall, narrow spaces. Once the adjoining house was gutted, it was fitted with a bilevel assemblage that has just a hint of solid walls at the mouth of the bedroom area.

Wood is the principal material in the new interior, a complement to the whitewashed brick walls.

ABOVE Generously scaled openings between the old house and its newly acquired neighbor dissolve the original boundaries between the two structures.

hovers in the space, seemingly solely supported in the air by a series of 4-ft. by 8-ft. beams.

Sheltered below is the master bedroom, a cozy place compared to the airy, sun-filled sitting room above. It has an ambience that might be described as "modern Zen cabin": a combination of rustic albeit pristine fir-wood construction and its precisely ordered, expressed structure. Timber posts and planks float away from each other as well as from the brick walls; slits and slots of daylight are visible around the perimeter of the room. A wide canvas roller shade can be pulled down to close off the space.

The bed is surrounded by a matrix of wooden bookshelves and flanked by two wardrobes, which are also enclosed by canvas panels. As the architect, Mark McInturff, points out, the arrangement is intentionally—and intriguingly—unclear: is the unit of bed/shelves/closets a large, multifunctional piece of furniture or is it a small piece of a building inserted into the space? The architecture provides the perfect venue for reflection on itself.

WINDOW WALLS

Soaring expanses of thick plate glass are a dramatic means to open up the wall and provide an unobstructed view, blurring the boundary between indoors and out. It's an ideal detail for modern homes. But for town houses of other styles, walls of windows might be a little too slick or commercial in appearance.

An approach that's more flexible in residential use is a mosaic of individual windows. They can be an assemblage of identical shapes or a grouping of different-size units mitered together. The composition can follow the lead of the architecture, perhaps paralleling the staggered rise of a stairway or the peak of a gable. Or it

can relate more to exterior elements: a vertical orientation to frame a stand of trees, for instance. Banding smaller windows together also provides an opportunity to mix fixed and operable units, allowing fresh air into the home and promoting cross-ventilation.

LEFT One way to make a basic space more evocative is by imbuing it with an ambiguous quality; people become curious about the room they're occupying. In the bedroom, for example, it's unclear whether its design is part of the building's structure or is simply a large piece of furniture.

The glazing itself is another variable in the window-wall equation, one that can be both decorative and serviceable. Laminated glass may be prescribed where strong winds are a concern. Energy regulations will most certainly affect the choice of materials as well; factory-applied coatings on the glass to control heat and light are generally undetectable from either side of the window. Mixing several types of glass together—as in David's residence, with its patchwork of sandblasted panes, colored glass, and clear glazing—makes the window wall more of a mediator of light and views than a direct, unfettered connection to the outdoors.

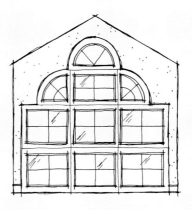

DIRECTORY OF ARCHITECTS